# Sustainability and Organizational Change Management

There is no bigger challenge for organizational change management in the contemporary world than achieving greater sustainability. The challenges associated with sustainable development are multifaceted, including criteria pertaining to the delivery of environmental, social, ethical and economic results. Creating sustainable value requires companies to address issues that relate to pollution and waste, created by industrialization; to respond in a transparent manner to the challenges increasingly raised by the civil society, namely NGOs; to invest in emerging technologies that provide innovative solutions to many of today's environmental problems and effectively to respond to the challenges of increased poverty and inequality around the globe. On the other hand, to create shareholder value, managers must focus not only on cost reduction and risk control but also on fostering innovation, enhancing corporate reputation within external stakeholders, and establishing a credible growth path for the future.

The current global financial crisis has left few untouched: unprecedented unemployment figures, public deficits, bankruptcies, redundancies, austerity regimes, and governments bailing out banks all over the globe. World confidence is at a record low. How can management scholars encounter solutions for the dilemmas created by this scenario of change in which they can manage to respond to change sustainably? This book provides some answers to these pressing questions.

This book was originally published as a special issue of the *Journal of Change Management.*

**Stewart R. Clegg** is Executive Director of the Centre for Management and Organization Studies and a member of the Management Discipline Group at the University of Technology, Sydney, Australia. He is also a Professor at Nova School of Economics and Business, Lisbon, Portugal, and Strategic Research Advisor at Newcastle University Business School, UK.

**João Amaro de Matos** is Associate Dean for International Development, PhD Program Director, and CEMS Director, at Nova School of Economics And Business, Lisbon, Portugal. He is also affiliated with the Getulio Vargas Foundation, São Paulo School of Business, Brazil.

# Sustainability and Organizational Change Management

*Edited by*

**Stewart R. Clegg and João Amaro de Matos**

LONDON AND NEW YORK

First published 2016
by Routledge
2 Park Square, Milton Park, Abingdon, Oxon, OX14 4RN, UK

and by Routledge
711 Third Avenue, New York, NY 10017, USA

First issued in paperback 2017

*Routledge is an imprint of the Taylor & Francis Group, an informa business*



*British Library Cataloguing in Publication Data*
A catalogue record for this book is available from the British Library

ISBN 13: 978-1-138-29486-8 (pbk)
ISBN 13: 978-1-138-94330-8 (hbk)

Typeset in Times New Roman
by RefineCatch Limited, Bungay, Suffolk

**Publisher's Note**
The publisher accepts responsibility for any inconsistencies that may have arisen during the conversion of this book from journal articles to book chapters, namely the possible inclusion of journal terminology.

# Contents

# Citation Information

The following chapters were originally published in the *Journal of Change Management*, volume 13, issue 4 (December 2013). When citing this material, please use the original page numbering for each article, as follows:

**Chapter 1**
*Sustainability and Organizational Change*
João Amaro de Matos & Stewart R. Clegg
*Journal of Change Management*, volume 13, issue 4 (December 2013)
pp. 382–386

**Chapter 2**
*The Public–Private Nexus in Organizational Economics and the Challenge of Sustainable Value Creation*
Christos N. Pitelis
*Journal of Change Management*, volume 13, issue 4 (December 2013)
pp. 387–406

**Chapter 3**
*The 'Why Not'–Perspective of Green Purchasing: A Multilevel Case Study Analysis*
Edeltraud Guenther, Anne-Karen Hueske, Kristin Stechemesser & Lioba Buscher
*Journal of Change Management*, volume 13, issue 4 (December 2013)
pp. 407–423

**Chapter 4**
*The Good, the Bad, and the Successful – How Corporate Social Responsibility Leads to Competitive Advantage and Organizational Transformation*
André Martinuzzi & Barbara Krumay
*Journal of Change Management*, volume 13, issue 4 (December 2013)
pp. 424–443

**Chapter 5**
*The Political Ecology of Palm Oil Production*
Renato J. Orsato, Stewart R. Clegg & Horacio Falcão
*Journal of Change Management*, volume 13, issue 4 (December 2013)
pp. 444–459

**Chapter 6**

*From the Physics of Change to Realpolitik: Improvisational Relations of Power and Resistance*
Miguel Pina e Cunha, Stewart R. Clegg, Arménio Rego & Joana Story
*Journal of Change Management*, volume 13, issue 4 (December 2013)
pp. 460–476

The following chapter was originally published in the *Journal of Change Management*, volume 9, issue 4 (December 2009). When citing this material, please use the original page numbering for each article, as follows:

**Chapter 7**

*Advancing Sustainability Through Change and Innovation: A Co-evolutionary Perspective*
Suzanne Benn & Ellen Baker
*Journal of Change Management*, volume 9, issue 4 (December 2009)
pp. 383–397

The following chapter was originally published in the *Journal of Change Management*, volume 12, issue 2 (June 2012). When citing this material, please use the original page numbering for each article, as follows:

**Chapter 8**

*A Proposed Model for Evaluating the Sustainability of Continuous Change Programmes*
Mikael Brännmark & Suzanne Benn
*Journal of Change Management*, volume 12, issue 2 (June 2012)
pp. 231–245

# Notes on Contributors

**Ellen Baker** is an Honorary Associate in Management at the University of Technology, Sydney, Australia. Her current research interests are networks and collaboration, innovation, and community development.

**Suzanne Benn** is Professor of Education for Sustainability and Director of the Australian Research Institute in Education for Sustainability, Graduate School of the Environment, Macquarie University, Sydney, Australia. Her research interests lie in learning and organizational change for sustainability, and corporate social responsibility.

**Mikael Brännmark** is based in the School of Technology and Health at the Royal Institute of Technology, Stockholm, Sweden.

**Lioba Buscher** received a PhD in Statistics from the University of Dortmund, Germany, and worked for several years at the Technische Universität Dresden, Germany. Her research interests are environmental and health economics.

**Stewart R. Clegg** is Executive Director of the Centre for Management and Organization Studies and a member of the Management Discipline Group at the University of Technology, Sydney, Australia. He is also a Professor at Nova School of Economics and Business, Lisbon, Portugal, and Strategic Research Advisor at Newcastle University Business School, UK.

**Miguel Pina e Cunha** is Professor at Nova School of Business and Economics, Lisbon, Portugal. His research interests include process-based views of organizations; the paradoxes of organizing; virtuous and toxic leadership; and the unfolding of positive and genocidal forms of organization.

**Horacio Falcão** is an Affiliate Professor of Decision Sciences at INSEAD, Singapore. He is also a co-founder of Pluris Pte. Ltd. His research interests revolve around the effectiveness of win-win/collaborative vs. win-lose/power negotiation moves; increasing ethics in negotiation while improving results; strategic organizational moves that enhance individual negotiation effectiveness; and cross-cultural negotiation dynamics among individuals and in the context of organizational change.

**Edeltraud Guenther** has been a Professor of Business Administration in the Chair of Environmental Management and Accounting at Technische Universität Dresden, Germany, since 1996. Her current research fields are environmental performance measurement; value-based management of environmental resources; hurdle analysis and the deceleration of consumption as well as production processes.

**Anne-Karen Hueske** is a Research Associate at the Chair of Environmental Management and Accounting at Technische Universität Dresden, Germany. Her research interest is on barriers to organizational change and innovation, especially in the biotechnology industry.

**Barbara Krumay** works at the Research Institute for Managing Sustainability, Vienna University of Economics and Business, Austria. Her research covers a broad variety of topics with a strong focus on ethical issues, such as privacy or corporate responsibility. Her main areas are corporate social responsibility; ICT and sustainability; and life-long learning.

**André Martinuzzi** is the Director of the Research Institute for Managing Sustainability, and Associate Professor, at Vienna University of Economics and Business, Austria. He has co-ordinated projects in the 5th, 6th and 7th EU Framework Programme, has conducted tendered research projects on behalf of six different EU DGs, Eurostat, the UN Development Programme and for several national ministries. His main areas of research are corporate sustainability; sustainable development policies; evaluation research and knowledge brokerage.

**João Amaro de Matos** is Associate Dean for International Development, PhD Program Director, and CEMS Director, at Nova School of Economics And Business, Lisbon, Portugal. He is also affiliated with the Getulio Vargas Foundation, São Paulo School of Business, Brazil.

**Renato J. Orsato** is a Professor in the São Paulo School of Management, Brazil, and Academic Director of the Centre for Sustainability Studies at the Getúlio Vargas Foundation in São Paulo, Brazil. He is the author of *Sustainability strategies: When does it pay to be green?* (2009), and was a finalist for the Academy of Management 2010 ONE Book Award. He has written several book chapters and teaching cases, and published in academic journals such as *California Management Review*, *Organization Studies*, *Journal of Cleaner Production*, and *Journal of Industrial Ecology*.

**Christos N. Pitelis** is Director of the Centre for International Business and Management, Reader in International Business and Competitiveness at the Judge Business School, and Fellow in Economics at Queens' College, University of Cambridge, UK. He is Editor of the *Cambridge Journal of Economics*, the *Collected Papers of Edith Penrose* and on the editorial boards of, among others, *Organization Science*, *Organization Studies* and *Management International Review*. He has researched, consulted, co-ordinated projects and provided executive education to business, governments and organizations, such as the European Commission; the United Nations; USAID; and the Commonwealth Secretariat.

**Arménio Rego** is an Assistant Professor at Universidade de Aveiro, Portugal. He has been published in journals such as *Applied Psychology: An International Review*, *Journal of Business Ethics*, *Journal of Business Research*, *Journal of Occupational Health Psychology*, *Leadership Quarterly*, and *Organization Studies*. His research deals mainly with positive organizational scholarship.

**Kristin Stechemesser** is a Research Associate at the Chair of Environmental Management and Accounting, at the Technische Universität Dresden, Germany. Her research interests are green procurement; climate change mitigation and adaptation; and organizational learning.

**Joana Story** is Assistant Professor at Nova School of Business and Economics, Lisbon, Portugal. She has published in several international journals including *Human Resource Management*, *International Human Resource Management Journal*, *Journal of Leadership and Organizational Studies*, and *Journal of Leadership Studies*. Her research interests include global leadership; leadership and management in emerging markets; ethical leadership; social responsibility; and organizational behaviour.

# Sustainability and Organizational Change†

JOÃO AMARO DE MATOS* & STEWART R. CLEGG*,**

*Nova School of Business and Economics, Lisbon, Portugal, **Centre for Management and Organization Studies, University of Technology, Sydney, Australia

There is no bigger challenge for organizational change management in the contemporary world than achieving greater sustainability. Challenges associated with sustainable development are multifaceted, including criteria pertaining to the delivery of environmental, social, ethical and economic results. Creating sustainable value requires companies to address issues that relate to pollution and waste, created by industrialization, to respond in a transparent manner to the challenges increasingly raised by civil society, namely NGOs, to invest in emerging technologies that provide innovative solutions to many of today's environmental problems and to respond effectively to the challenges of increased poverty and inequality around the globe. On the other hand, to create shareholder value, managers must focus not only on cost reduction and risk control but also on fostering innovation, enhancing corporate reputation within external stakeholders and establishing a credible growth path for the future.

The need for sustainable development is the major organizational change that contemporary businesses face. For almost the entire trajectory of industrial organizations its material basis has been dependent on the exploitation of nature with consequent external effects, such as the despoliation of nature. Only in recent times has this major organizational change begun to percolate into business organizations' strategies and those of governments. That such organizational change is recognized to be both major and transcendent can be seen in the increased attention several different institutions, such as the European Union (EU), now pay to issues of sustainability. The EU developed the strategy for 'Europe 2020',

†The initial call for papers for a Special Issue of the *Journal of Change Management* was announced in conjunction with the 1st CEMS Annual Event Research Symposium, which was held in Lisbon, hosted by Nova School of Business and Economics, on 8 December 2011. The theme of the Special Issue was devoted to *Sustainability as a Real Opportunity: How Can Management Foster What Politics Cannot?*

based on three pillars: new sources for new growth, reaching out for a sustainable society and going green for a competitive economy.

The EU is seeking to shape major organizational changes towards sustainability in difficult, dangerous and interesting times. The world is coming out of its worst financial and economic crisis since the 1920s. The crisis has left few untouched: unprecedented unemployment figures, public deficits, bankruptcies, redundancies and governments bailing out banks all over the globe. World confidence is at a record low. How can management scholars contribute and analyse solutions for the dilemmas of managing to change sustainably?

In this call for papers, we invited researchers to consider the intersection of the demands both to create shareholder value and ensure sustainable development and to present their research work on this topic. We received contributions from many different management areas, from marketing to finance, from human resources to entrepreneurship. All papers were double blind reviewed and in every case subject to revision and resubmission following review.

From the papers submitted, we eventually chose five for publication. The Special Issue leads in with a contribution from Cambridge strategist and industrial economist, Christos Pitelis, on 'The Public-Private Nexus in Organizational Economics and the Challenge of Sustainable Value Creation.' In this paper, he explores the scope for cross-fertilization between extant alternative organizational economics perspectives on the private-public nexus. Organizational economics has been one of the more laggard areas of analysis in terms of its interest in issues of sustainability. It is because organizational economics as a perspective has been slow to develop a focus on sustainable organizational change that this paper is a particularly useful contribution, in which the comparative advantages of apparently competing perspectives are elaborated and the opportunities for synthesis explored, particularly in their implications for public–private links that foster sustainable system-wide value creation. It is precisely these kinds of links that will be necessary to create meta-level changes that the global agenda for sustainability will require. To do so, the limitations of organizational economics as a whole need to be transcended through leveraging a multi- and cross-disciplinary perspective.

The second contribution comes from members of the Faculty of Business and Economics of The Technische Universitaet, Dresden. The contributors are Edeltraud Guenther, Anne-Karen Hueske, Kristin Stechemesser, and Lioba Buscher. These authors present a paper on 'The "Why Not"-Perspective of Green Purchasing: A Multilevel Case Study Analysis'. A vital part of the change programmes that make organizations more sustainable are the decisions that they make when purchasing. It is all too easy to externalize a lack of sustainability into the supply chain while representing the organization itself as highly sustainable. The focal organization can claim that it has changed by becoming more sustainable in its practices, but if it does so by externalizing unsustainable elements of organizational behaviour into the supply chain there may well be no net benefit. The result may be 'green-washing' an appearance of change rather than the achievement of real organizational change.

The paper begins by noting that organizations that seek to change by becoming greener need not only a normative and instrumental 'how to do it' perspective but also a perspective on 'why not', focusing on factors that may hamper, decelerate or even block green purchasing. The paper presents the results of a case study that follows Eisenhardt's well-known design for case study research. The analysis is of the procurement strategies of six European municipal organizations that are attempting to go green. In the first stage of the project, the authors analysed barriers to green procurement in these six municipalities across five European countries; in the second stage, they combined those findings with the literature on multilevel research, presenting a framework based on a multilevel categorization. The authors developed hypotheses by analysing both the organizational and the individual level in one of the biggest procurement agencies in Europe.

Due to its critical gatekeeper position in organizations, the focus was on the procurement process. If procurement practices do change organizationally then whatever changes may occur towards more sustainable practices within the focal organizations will be undercut by behaviour elsewhere in the supply chain. The research question that they address is 'Why do organizations *not* implement green purchasing?' Researching organizational change through analysis of non-decision-making has a strong lineage in social science (see, e.g. Crenson, 1971). The authors answer the question through a multilevel analysis examining the relationships that lead to barriers for green purchasing as these are constituted between the individual, group, organizational level and the external environment. Complementing the 'how to' perspective with taking the 'why not perspective' the authors identify the challenges facing managers who foster organizational change programmes for sustainability.

André Martinuzzi and Barbara Krumay present 'The Good, the Bad, and the Successful – How CSR Leads to Competitive Advantage and Organizational Transformation.' In this paper they link the adoption of corporate social responsibility (CSR) as a major change to four key areas of organizational change management. The focus is on changes in project management, quality management and strategic management, as well as in organizational learning and transformation.

They develop a stage model for CSR implementation. This stage model represents a referential framework that supports the analysis of the materiality of CSR, the potential of CSR to create competitive advantage, and the impacts of CSR on business and society. A comprehensive literature review of material on CSR provides the frame for investigation of specific business operations as well as a series of case studies in the textile sector and the chemical industry. They suggest that companies try to cope with new societal demands by integrating them into well-established business operations: they change but do so buy integration and renovation rather than revolutionary action. Often they will choose to pursue change strategies in an area perceived as 'good' by the public, making use of project management know-how to do so. In these cases, this is organizational change in the 'shop window' while behind the scenes things stay pretty much the same because these 'good' projects are not necessarily linked to the companies' core activities. Many companies also implement CSR through quality management to avoid 'bad things'. Here organizational change is focused on quality and the elimination of waste. Although quality management systems can and do have sustainability implications by reducing waste and thus increasing efficiency the processes that deliver them are often seen as annoying obligations, with a low stimulus for innovation resulting. The changes that occur, in other words, make for more economical presentation of the shop window, but do not represent widespread organizational change.

It is only at the level of strategic CSR that larger scale organizational change for sustainability occurs. Strategic CSR perceives opportunities for innovation through sustainability, despite well-established structures, processes and thought patterns that counter innovative thinking and acting. Transformational CSR tries to overcome these constraints by linking CSR with organizational learning that can foster system-wide change. There are real practitioner implications for change management in this work. Companies can use it to assess the stage they have reached in managing organizational changes in CSR implementation, strive for higher impact, boost their competitiveness and be seen to change towards greater CSR maturity.

In a paper that focuses on East Asia and one of its major agribusinesses, palm oil, authored by Renato Orsato, Stewart Clegg and Horacio Falcão, the politics of organizational change in terms of sustainability is tackled head on. The paper addresses 'The Political Ecology of Palm Oil Production: Eco-activism and Multinationals in Malaysia and Indonesia.' The study is based on extensive fieldwork in the island of Borneo and offers an analysis of the different levels in the global value chain of the palm oil industry, including local organizations, the industry structure overall, as well as the local governments of Malaysia and Indonesia.

The palm oil industry produces what is now the world's leading crop export. Palm oil production is an area that is ecologically and socially destructive. It also lies at the end of a value chain that stretches into some of the largest and most successful multinational organizations in the Western world, many of which make claims to being sustainable in their marketing. The production of palm oil is at the base of the supply chain that reaches into our bathrooms and our kitchens.

Palm oil production is a highly contested terrain. It is a plantation crop, mass-produced, in areas of the tropics that have been stripped of biodiversity and turned over to plantation style monoculture. Such strategies for economic development have many critics of the organizational changes that these strategies produce on the ecologies, economies and societies in question. These criticisms have surfaced organizationally in disputes that have been aired in and around the Roundtable on Sustainable Palm Oil, a type of voluntary environmental initiative, or green club, as they have also been called.

The use of the political ecology framework for the analysis of the palm oil industry contributes not only to the development of a more institutional power perspective on organizational change management but also provides solid ground for analysis of green clubs, which are an increasingly important type of organization used by managers globally to manage sustainability, and impressions of it, as a key aspect of organizational change.

The Special Issue concludes with another paper that focuses on the politics of change and which, in so doing, revisits the most debated area in change management – resistance to it. Miguel Pinha e Cuhna, Stewart Clegg, Armenio Rego, and Joana Story offer an analysis that charts the shift 'From the Physics of Change to Realpolitik: Improvisational Relations of Power and Resistance.'

The paper addresses one of the key staples of the change management field: resistance to change. Dominant tendencies in the managerialist literature, ever since Coch and French's (1948) famous article, have tended to see resistance to change as something irrational. The authors problematize mechanistic action–reaction types of analyses, in which change and resistance to change are counter-posed. In doing so they uncover some fragility in debates that differentiate between the agents of change and resisters of change. The paper addresses the roles attached to the participants in change processes. Beyond the traditional separation between agents and recipients of change, the paper suggests the potential of minimal structures and improvisations as means for achieving change. Improvisation, they suggest, creates a space in which established orders of organizing are challenged and alternative orders are allowed to flourish. Hence, if organizational change is to occur, it is more likely to be adopted and less likely to be resisted where it is not seen as something imposed but instead is emergent. The authors suggest that, paradoxically, directed structural interventions can produce organizational contexts more amenable to fostering emergent change. These systematic change management programmes should seek to minimize structure, shift roles and combine paradoxical requirements, helping not only to diffuse resistance to change but also serving to recreate the nature of change in organizations. In this way, to use a previous metaphor, change that goes beyond the shop window is more likely to occur.

Overall, these papers provide informed and constructive insight into an area of debate that is often occluded in corporate spin and critical controversy. Greenwash aplenty accompanies many practices of managing organizational change that claim to be moving the organization towards a greener and more sustainable future, as authors such as Banerjee (2009) has argued. If there is to be real progress made in managing organizations on this planet then tackling issues of sustainability effectively must be at the forefront of concerns for advancing both the theory and practice of change.

## References


Banerjee, B. S. (2009). Corporate social responsibility: The good, the bad and the ugly. *Critical Sociology, 34*(1), 51–79.

Coch, L., & French, J. R. P., Jr. (1948). Overcoming resistance to change. *Human Relations, 1*(4), 512–532.

Crenson, M. (1971). *The un-politics of air pollution: A study of non-decisionmaking in the cities*. Baltimore, MD: Johns Hopkins University Press.

# The Public – Private Nexus in Organizational Economics and the Challenge of Sustainable Value Creation

CHRISTOS N. PITELIS

*Judge Business School and Queens' College, University of Cambridge, UK*

ABSTRACT *This article explores the scope for cross-fertilization between extant alternative organizational economics perspectives on the private – public nexus. It is suggested that there is substantial scope, which has gone underexplored. The comparative advantages are highlighted, and a synthesis and extension of apparently competing perspectives is provided. Furthermore, the article explores the implications for public – private links that foster sustainable system-wide value creation and concludes by pinpointing limitations of organizational economics as a whole and the need to leverage a multi- and cross-disciplinary perspective.*

## Introduction

In this paper the substantive aim is to address public-private-polity links that foster sustainable system-wide efficiency-value creation. Conceptually, the paper explores the scope for cross-fertilization between alternative organizational economics perspectives on the public-private-polity nexus. While organizational economics is one approach only, it has been influential in the analysis of both private and public organization. Yet, recent conceptual advances in the analysis of business organization and strategy have not been leveraged for the analysis of public organization. We aim to explore this issue and in so doing, we attempt an integration of alternative organizational economics perspectives on business and public organization, and provide a critical synthesis and extension on their interrelationship. We then explore their implications for the type of public–private links that promote sustainable system-wide efficiency-value creation. Finally, we highlight limitations of economics-based thinking and call for a cross-disciplinary dialogue.

The first section discusses alternative theories of private (business and industry-wide) organization. The following section discusses economic theories of public organization, particularly economic theories of the state. The third section explores their interrelationships, commonalities and differences, the scope for a critical synthesis and extension, and their implications for public–private links that foster system-wide efficiency and value creation. The last section highlights limitations and concludes.

## Alternative Organizational Economic Perspectives on Private Organization

### *The Efficient Resource Allocation-Market Failure-based Theory-Industrial Organization and Transaction Costs-based Views*

Numerous scholars have developed the major elements of the efficient resource allocation-market failure-based theory (MFT) over many years (Freeman, 2004). The basic tenets are expounded in Alfred Marshall's 1920 *Principles of Economics*. While Marshall had a rather nuanced approach to firms and their internal operations and capabilities (Harcourt & Kriesler, 2012), subsequent developments in microeconomics and industrial organization (IO) economics focused on the industry as the unit of analysis (Pepall, Richards, & Norman, 2008). The main economic question raised by this perspective is how the price–output decisions or equilibria of firms operating in industries (collection of firms producing similar products, such as cars) impact on the efficient allocation of scarce resources and on the optimality of the market system as a whole.

The method used to answer this question involves the assumption of 'optimizing behaviour' by economic agents – firms are assumed to maximize profits. Given this objective, all one needs in order to determine the price–output 'equilibrium' in an industry is knowledge of the cost structure, the demand conditions and the type of industry structure, which can be perfectly or imperfectly competitive. 'Perfect competition' exists when firms are numerous, produce homogenous products and there exists free entry and exit in the industry. Under these assumptions firms can only make 'normal' (or zero economic) profits; that is they will simply cover their average costs (defined to include compensation for all factors of production, including managers and entrepreneurs).

'Imperfect competition' refers to all types of non-perfectly competitive markets, such as monopoly (a single seller in the industry) or oligopoly (relatively few sellers whose actions have an impact on each other – there exists interdependence). A limiting case of oligopoly is duopoly (two firms in the industry). In the case of imperfect competition, profit maximizing behaviour often leads to prices in excess of the perfectly competitive ones, and hence to super-normal or 'monopoly profits'.

A problem with monopoly is that in order to maximize profits, monopolies need to restrict output. This leads to lower levels of output than is possible under perfect competition, leading to underutilization (misallocation) of scarce resources, the anathema of neoclassical microeconomics. That is why this approach regards monopoly as bad. It represents a structural market failure and needs to be addressed (see below).

Monopoly and perfect competition are two extremes; in practice most industries will tend to be imperfectly competitive-oligopolistic. Analysing oligopolies is more exciting but not as straightforward. Given the many possibilities available for the possible behaviour of oligopolies, there exist many oligopoly models (Pepall et al., 2008; Tirole, 1988).

In the absence of perfect competition, there exists scope for the government to step in to restore perfectly competitive conditions. A problem is that absent perfect competition across all industries in the economy intervention in one market is not guaranteed to improve efficiency (the problem of 'second best'), except under rather restrictive assumptions (Gilbert & Newbery 1982). This limits the power of IO to provide useful public policy prescription, which is its purported aim, see Hunt (2000).

Related problems of the MFT include restrictive assumptions, such as perfect information/knowledge, optimizing behaviour, inter-firm co-operation being seen mostly as price collusion and technology/innovations being exogenous. In this context perfect competition implies the absence of rivalry. In addition, the focus on efficient allocation of scarce resources underplays resource-wealth creation. While changes in resource allocation can lead to changes in resource creation, it is far from evident that a particular efficient resource allocation at any given time is the only (let alone the best) way to affect resource creation (Pitelis, 2012b). Indeed resource creation is automatically related to inter-temporal issues, which poses another problem for the MFT – its focus is on comparative statics, not on inter-temporal efficiency. The last mentioned involves knowledge and innovation, which the MFT considers to be exogenous.

The difficulties of the MFT to deal with inter-temporal efficiency (the theme of the founding father of economics Adam Smith and many leading economists since, such as Joseph Schumpeter) led IO scholars such as Baumol (1991) to lament the sub-optimal properties of 'perfect competition' with regard to innovation and hence dynamic inter-temporal economic performance. A reason, Baumol observed, echoing Schumpeter (1942), is that the assumptions of both these types of market structure remove any incentive to innovate.

The realism and usefulness of the IO perspective, especially for policy-makers, has been questioned both from within and from without mainstream economics. From within, 'managerial theories' drew on Berle and Means' (1932) statement of separation of ownership from control to claim that controlling professional managers maximize their own utility rather than profits. Such utility includes maximizing sales, discretionary expenditures, growth and other interests (Marris, 1996). Subsequent developments have tried to address the resultant problem of 'agency' (Alchian & Demsetz, 1972; Jensen & Meckling, 1976). The emergent 'agency' literature gradually became the foundation of the 'shareholder value' approach to corporate governance (Lazonick & O'Sullivan, 2000). In this literature, the fact that agents could pursue interests not necessarily defined by the interests of the owners of capital is a problem that can be solved by making agents' interests more aligned with those of capital owners through, for example, granting them significant stock options as a part of their total remuneration. The result is a focus on shareholder value, but it is one that privileges short-term accounting over longer-term innovation and investment that might reduce short-term profits (Klein, Mahoney, McGahan, & Pitelis, 2012a).

To conclude, MFT has a long history of distinction and frustration. Its concepts and models have proven resilient, influential and of import for other disciplines. Fundamental and influential ideas have emerged through them and their criticism that has helped further the appreciation of organizations, markets and economies (Winter, 2012). To date there exists no alternative explanation of price – output decisions by firms operating in industries, of equal generality and rigour. In its Porterian version, MFT has informed management theory and managerial practice (Porter, 1991). It is important, however, to look at MFT as it is – an abstraction, potentially dangerous when taken at face value. Last but not least, it is not clear whether more or less progress could have been made in organizational economics scholarship, were the MFT – IO approach not so dominant.

A challenge to the IO approach was Coase's (1937) transaction costs perspective. This is still a market failure-based approach; only now market failure is seen as 'natural' (not structural) and attributable to high market transaction costs. In addition, the private firm is seen as a device that can solve market failure, by internalizing market transactions. Where markets cannot deliver because of barriers to transactional efficiency, organizational hierarchies are said to emerge as a solution to market imperfections.

In Coase's (1937) article, the nature of the firm was considered in terms of the 'employment contract' between an entrepreneur and labourers. Coase observed that the employment contract firm could have advantages in terms of transaction costs. As intra-firm transactions also involve costs, the internalization of market transactions will take place up to the point where the transaction costs involved in having a transaction organized by the market are equal to the intra-firm transaction (organizational) costs of undertaking this transaction intra-firm. Accordingly the nature and boundaries of the firm can be explained in terms of overall market and organizational costs minimization.

The development of Coase's work, mainly by Williamson (1975, 1985), focused on asset specificity (assets, the redeployment of which involves loss of value) as the driver of integration (in particular, vertically) but also through conglomerate diversification and cross-border expansion (Williamson, 1991). Coase questioned the importance of asset specificity and also later expressed regrets for his almost exclusive focus on the 'employment relationship', claiming that one should focus on the (Coasean) nature of the firm but also on its essence, which is 'running a business'. In his view, this involves more than the employment contracts and includes the use of non-human resources and one's own time and capabilities to produce for a profit (Coase, 1991).

Despite extensive literature on transaction costs that includes support and criticisms (see David & Han, 2004, for an assessment of the evidence, which is mixed), Coase's distinction between the 'nature' and the 'essence' was little noticed. Subsequent developments zeroed in on 'property rights' (Grossman & Hart, 1986; Hart, 1995) and problems of metering and (self)-monitoring

(Alchian & Demsetz, 1972) to address the question of the existence and scope of the firm as well as why capital employs labour rather than the other way around. The answer provided was couched in terms of the efficiency benefits of property rights and the need for (self)-monitoring, in the context of team production: see Kim and Mahoney (2002), Pitelis (2007), Klein et al. (2012a), for more detailed critical assessments and syntheses. None of these theories attempted to deal with Coase's 'essence' of the firm, which is 'running a business'.

### *The Resource Creation Perspective: Resource, Capabilities, Evolutionary and System-based Views*

Contributions by Demsetz (1988) and Nelson and Winter (1982) as well as the emergence of the resource-based view (RBV) drew on earlier works by Simon (1955), Cyert and March (1963), Demsetz (1973) and Edith Penrose (1959) (see among others Barney, 1991; Mahoney & Pandian 1992; Peteraf, 1993; Teece, 1982; Wernerfelt, 1984; for the RBV, and Winter 2012, for a recent account of the evolutionary view), and went some way towards explicating what firms do, thus addressing in part the problem of the 'essence' of the firm. A critical concern, for example, of the strategy literature is to explain how firms aim to acquire sustainable competitive advantage (SCA) (see for example Lippman & Rumelt, 2003; Peteraf & Barney, 2003; Pitelis, 2009b; Teece, 2007). This involves issues pertaining to 'running a business'. For example, in the RBV, the diagnosis, building, re-configuration and leveraging of intra-firm resources that are valuable, rare, inimitable and non-substitutable help firms acquire SCAs. This is at least part and parcel of Coase's 'essence' (Pitelis & Teece, 2009, 2010).

The lineage of the evolutionary, resource and capabilities perspectives includes founding fathers in economics, such as Smith (1776) and Marx (1959). Smith and Marx focused on wealth creation, not just resource allocation. They both saw competition as a process, regulating prices and profit rates, not as a type of market structure. Smith described the productivity gains achievable through specialization, the division of labour, the generation of skills and inventions within the (pin) factory. Marx also suggested there is a dialectical relation between monopoly and competition (whereby competition leads to monopoly and monopoly can only maintain itself through the competitive struggle) and stressed the impact of this relationship on technological change, the rate of profit and the 'laws of motion' of capitalism at large. Marx focused, in addition, on competition (conflict) within the factory, and in the society at large, between employers and employees, between Capital and Labour. Building critically on Marx, Schumpeter (1942) described competition as a process of creative destruction through innovations. He saw monopoly as a necessary and just (yet only temporary) reward for innovations that bestowed initial advantages. He attributed firms' differential performance to differential innovativeness and saw concentration to be the result of such innovativeness.

In Penrose's (1959) book, 'The Theory of the Growth of the Firm', firms are seen as bundles of resources in which interaction generates knowledge, which releases resources. 'Excess resources' are an incentive to management for (endogenous) growth and innovation as they can be put to use at almost zero marginal cost (since they have already been employed and their release is hindered by indivisibilities). Differential innovations and growth lead to concentration, which, however, can also be maintained through monopolistic practices. The economic world is seen as one of big business competition, where competition is god and the devil at the same time. It drives innovativeness, yet it is through its restrictions that monopoly profit can be maintained.

Building on Penrose, Richardson (1972) observed that firms compete but also co-operate extensively. Such cooperation is not just a case of price collusion, as the neoclassical theory assumes but sits structurally between market and hierarchy, something that occurs when firm activities are complementary but dissimilar (require different capabilities).

Elsewhere, developing the behavioural theory of the firm, Simon (1947) and March and Simon (1958) questioned the very notion of 'Olympian' all-seeing rationality, proposing instead that 'bounded' (limited, procedural) rationality was a more appropriate heuristic for organizational decision-making. March and Simon (1958) doubted whether decision-makers really look for optimal solutions. They suggested that they look for 'satisficing' solutions. Because of the limited capacity of human information processing, no one could consider all solutions and then decide which one was the best one – not even a top manager. But top managers, because of their wide experiences, have a repository of comparable cases to draw on for most decision situations, and on the basis of that limited search are able to be rational within the bounds of their own experiences. However, having more experience, these bounds are less constraining than would be the case were lower-order members to do the deciding. A careful analysis of all available information would be impossibly time-consuming, given that time (and motivation for such use of time) is a scarce resource. It is for this reason too that satisfactory decisions will be made rather than optimal ones. Simon and March saw people as having 'bounded rationality'. By this they meant to establish a distinction with the conception of economic rationalism that was inherent to the orthodox views of economics. The economic view of rationality assumed that the person would make rational decisions based on perfect knowledge about the nature of the phenomenon. This perfect knowledge would be contained in what economists call 'price signals', because all that you would need to know about broadly similar goods in perfectly competitive markets is how much they cost. A rational person would always buy the cheapest product, all other things being constant. This would be the optimal decision. But in complex organizations, Simon and March argued, decision-makers work under constraints that make optimal decisions impossible. They have imperfect knowledge because there is insufficient time to collect all the data they need, their information processing capacities are subject to cognitive limitations, they are not sure what they need to know and so on. The result is that rationality is 'bounded' and decision-makers cannot optimize but must 'satisfice' – make the best decisions that they can – those that are most satisfactory, based on the information available there and then. These views build on Cyert and March (1963), who focused on intra-organizational conflict, which could ensue from the articulation of different rationalities by different interests within and around the firm. In turn, these ideas reach back into the work of Weber (1947) and his focus on the constellation of interests that develops on a formally free market and how these can align or conflict with established authority that allocates the right to command and the duty to obey.

Cohen, March, and Olsen (1972) pushed March and Simon's critique one step further, announcing that the rationality of the decision-making process in organizations is organized according to the logic of what they call the garbage can. As they argue provocatively, decisions are made when solutions, problems, participants and choices flow around and coincide at a certain point. Like garbage in a can, these adjacencies are often purely random. Starbuck (1983) turned this logic completely upside down and argued that organizations are not so much problem solvers as action generators. Instead of analysing and deciding rationally how to solve problems, organizations spend most of their time generating problems to which they already have the solutions embedded in routines. It is much more economical that way. They know how to do what they will do, so all they have to do is work out why they will do it.

Building on a similar focus and highlighting the importance of routines, Nelson and Winter (1982) developed ideas currently of import to the resource-capabilities-based view. 'Routines', simultaneously encapsulate firms' unique package of knowledge, skills and competences, allowing them to operate in an evolving environment with a degree of path-dependent institutionalization that does not necessarily rely on continuous re-design, and passes on the evolving 'routines' to the also evolving organization (Winter, 2012).

Early contributions in the RBV did not aim also to explain the nature of the firm (Barney, 2001; Priem & Butler, 2001). The Penrosean version of the RBV, however, could be interpreted as a theory of the nature of the firm. The superiority of firms in terms of knowledge creation, innovation, endogenous growth and productivity, for production for sale in the market for a profit (attributed by Penrose to learning by doing and teamwork in the context of the cohesive shell of the organization), could be seen as an alternative and complementary to Coase's transaction cost-based explanation of the employment relationship, thus the nature and boundary of firms (Pitelis, 2002).

It is arguable that the most relevant recent development of the Coasean 'essence' of the firm is the dynamic capabilities (DCs) perspective (Eisenhardt & Martin, 2000; Helfat & Winter, 2011; Helfat et al., 2007; Katkalo, Pitelis, & Teece, 2010; Teece, 2007; Teece, Pisano, & Shuen, 1997). While Penrose (1959), Richardson (1972) and resource-based scholars used the concept of capabilities to explain the growth, scope and boundaries of firms as well as the institutional division of labour between market, firm and inter-firm cooperation (Richardson, 1972), they have not gone far enough in terms of analysing how firms can leverage these resources and capabilities so as to obtain SCA, in the context of uncertainty and radical change. Additionally there has been limited discussion of the nature and types of capabilities that can help engender SCA. This has been the agenda of the DCs perspective. By focusing on DCs as those higher-order capabilities that help create, re-configure and leverage those more basic, such as operational efficiencies (Helfat et al., 2007) and organizational resources, and by identifying the sensing and seizing of opportunities as well as the need to maintain SCA as key objective and functions of DCs, the DC perspective has arguably been a major advance in terms of explicating Coase's 'essence' of the firm (Katkalo et al., 2010).

The transaction costs and resource-capabilities views explain the emergence of more concentrated industry structures in terms of transaction costs and/or productivity-related efficiencies. In the transaction costs view, integration strategies can lead to more concentrated industry structures but through a reduction in transaction costs. Similarly, firm heterogeneity in the RBV can explain firm-level SCA, thus providing a reason why more efficient firms can grow faster, increasing industry concentration. Despite such similarities, however, the RBV and DCs also differ in many significant respects from both the IO and transaction costs perspectives. In particular, despite differences, these perspectives share the view that competition is not a type of market structure and that both the efficient allocation of scarce resources and the creation and capture of value and wealth (Pitelis, 2009b) are important. Efficient resource allocation through perfectly competitive market structures, moreover, is not seen as the best, let alone the only, way to foster value and wealth creation and capture.

The focus on the evolutionary and RBV on change, limited and bounded rationality, knowledge, innovation and learning as well as its 'systemic' (as opposed to market) perspective has arguably facilitated the emergence of a shift in the economic analysis of firms, business and industry organization, one that emphasizes the knowledge and innovation-promoting potential of different institutional configurations. The 'national', regional and sectoral systems of innovation approach, the literature on clusters of firms and the work of Porter (1990) on national competitiveness as well as the varieties of capitalism perspective (Hall & Soskice, 2001) draw upon and relate to the evolutionary/resource system-based view (see Wignaraja, 2003; Edquist, 2005; Lundvall, 2007; Pitelis, 2009a, 2012c, for various contributions).

Other implications of the resource-capabilities, evolutionary and systems-based perspective involve the following. First, the focus on value and wealth creation suggests a broader welfare criterion than just efficiency of resource allocation. Second, superior capabilities provide another efficiency-based reason for concentrated industry structures. Third, competition as a dynamic process of creative destruction through innovation points to a need to account for the determinants to innovate, when considering the effects of 'monopoly' but also, more widely, including business organization and strategy. Fourth, competition with cooperation (co-opetition), as in Richardson, implies the need to account for the potential productivity benefits of co-opetition, in devising business strategy and public policies. All these have important implications for the private–public nexus.

## Economic Theories of Public (State) Organization and the Public–Private Nexus

### *Economic Theories of the State*

The state is widely acknowledged to be a most important institutional device for resource allocation and creation along with the market and the firm (Freeman, 2004; Pitelis, 1991). Many theories have tried to explain the growth of the public sector in market economies (the so-called Wagner's Law) originating from a number of different perspectives. In brief, neoclassical theories considered such growth as a result of increasing demand for state services by sovereign consumers, while 'public choice' theorists regarded it as a result of state officials, politicians and bureaucrats' utility-maximizing policies, in a version of agency-type arguments (Mueller, 2006). In the Marxist tradition, the growth of the state is linked to the laws of motion of capitalism – increasing concentration and centralization of capital and declining profit rates generate simultaneous demands by capital and labour on the state to enhance their relative distributional shares, for example, through infrastructure provisions and increased welfare services, respectively. The state becomes an object of class struggle in which the policies that emerge reflect a balance of power between Capital and Labour that is constantly shifting with political economic and ideological conjunctures (Clegg, Boreham, & Dow, 1986). In addition, there is the question of the shifting alignment of state agents with these (Pusey 1991).

There are variations on these views within each school as well as other views from institutional, feminist and post-Keynesian perspectives (Hay, Lister, & Marsh, 2006; Pressman, 2006). Besides explaining why states increase their economic involvement over time, many economists in the 1980s focused their attention on why states fail to allocate resources efficiently and, more particularly, on the relative efficiency properties of market versus non-market resource allocation. Particularly well known here are the views of the Chicago School, in particular Friedman (1962) and Stigler (1988). Friedman emphasized the possibility of states becoming captive to special interests of powerful organized groups, notably business and trade unions. In addition, Stigler pointed to often-unintentional inefficiencies involved in cases of state intervention. Examples are re-distributional programmes by the state that dissipate more resources (for example in administrative costs) than they redistribute. For these reasons as well as the tendency generated by utility-maximizing bureaucrats and politicians towards excessive growth and rising and redundant costs, there is a long-term tendency leading to government failure. Wolf (1979) provided a classification of such failures in terms of derived externalities (the Stigler argument), rising and redundant costs because of officials' holding 'more is better' attitudes and distributional inequities that result from the powerful pressure groups.

At a wider conceptual level, the case for private ownership and market allocation is based on three theories. First, the property rights school suggests that communal ownership characterized by a lack of individual property rights will lead to dissipation – the 'tragedy of the commons'. Second, there is Hayek's (1945) view of dispersed knowledge, according to which knowledge is so widely dispersed in every society that efficient acquisition and utilization of such knowledge can be achieved only through price signals provided by markets – a precursor of crowdsourcing! Third, Alchian and Demsetz's (1972) residual claimant's theory suggests, much in line with the property rights school, that private ownership of firms is predicated on the need for a residual claimant of income-generating assets, in the absence of which members of a coalition would tend to free ride, thus leading to inefficient utilization of resources (Pitelis & Clarke, 1993).

There is a large literature on the merits and limitations of these theories (Eggertsson, 1990; Pitelis & Clarke, 1993). Some weaknesses have been exposed in each defence of private ownership and market allocation. Concerning the 'tragedy of the commons', it has been observed that, historically, communal ownership could have efficiency-enhancing effects (Ostrom, 2011). Hayek's critique of pure planning loses its force when one considers choices of degree between market and plan in 'mixed economies'. The residual claimant theory downplays the potential incentive-enhancing attributes of co-operatives and, moreover, becomes weaker when applied to modern joint-stock companies run by a controlling management group as well as when it is applied to knowledge workers (Klein et al., 2012a, Klein, Mahoney, McGahan, & Pitelis, 2013).

The Marxist theory paid particular attention to the theory of the state. Views here range from the instrumentalist theory (Miliband, 1969), which sees the state as an instrument of capital, through the structuralist perspective for which the necessity of capitalist cohesion, given the competitive struggle between different fractions of Capital, can only be achieved through the state (Poulantzas, 1969). In addition, there is the capital logic or state form derivation debate, where the state is seen as an outcome of the very logic of capital accumulation (Holloway & Picciotto, 1978), functioning as an 'ideal total capitalist'.

Variations apart, all Marxist theories view the state's existence and functions as the result of a quest and/or need to nurture the class interests of the capitalist class. Hymer (in Cohen, Felton, Van Liere, & Nikosi, 1979) has a historical justification of this need-quest. Marxists, most notably O'Connor (1973), also acknowledge the possibility of government (capitalist state) failure, but attributed it to a structural gap between receipts and outlays. Some Marxist ideas can be translated into mainstream terms, such as government failure. Always different is the focus on a distributional, class-based perspective, as opposed to the efficiency focus of the neoclassical mainstream. Some predictions by the Marxist School, for example the fiscal crisis and the 'austerity consensus', seem very relevant today in view of sovereign failures in Europe and elsewhere (Pitelis, 1991, 2012a).

### *Private – Public Links in Extant Organizational Economic Theory*

As noted the neoclassical economic perspective considers the state to be a result of market failure. In Smith (1776) the state was required mainly for the provision of justice and public works. More recent accounts pointed to prisoner's dilemma, coordination, asymmetric information and missing linkages-related market failures (Hardin, 1997; Rodrik, 2009). Coase (1960) and Arrow (1970) generalized the neoclassical perspective of instances of market failure leading to the state, in terms of transaction costs. This has been taken up and extended by North (1981) and Pitelis (1991).

There is limited discussion in the mainstream economics literature of the relationship between the firm and the state. Coase (1960) mentioned that firm and market transactions have to take place within the general legal framework imposed by the state. The implication is that firms and markets (the private sector) are seen as complements to the state. This implies a need for an explanation of the state in terms of private sector (not just market) failure. This leaves unresolved the question of why states do not substitute (replace) markets and firms (the private sector); i.e. why there is a market and not central planning. An explanation can be offered in terms of the – nowadays popular – concept of government failure, generalized in terms of transaction costs but also in terms of Coase's claim that in market economies the optimal mix between market and plan emerges endogenously and not from the top down (Coase, 1960), hence it is more efficient-desirable.

The major alternative to the mainstream neoclassical tradition on the private–public nexus is the Marxist. Regarding the *raison d'être* of the firm, the major contribution was Marglin's (1974). Developed independently of Williamson's perspective on markets and hierarchies, Marglin's ideas represent the major alternative to the transaction cost-efficiency argument. For Marglin, the main reason for the rise of the factory system, and thus the firm, from the previously existing putting-out system where merchants coordinated a series of market-based transactions with cottage-based industry, was the result of capitalist attempts to increase control over labour, to minimize pilferage and maximize effort. In this sense, the emergence of the firm in the factory system was due to control-distribution reasons. Any efficiency gains resulting from increased control should be seen as the outcome but not as the driving force. In addition, the process was often assisted by the state, acting in the interest of the emerging merchant-capitalist (Hymer, in Cohen et al., 1979). In this context the public–private nexus basically involves collusive behaviour between Capital and State for the joint appropriation of social value (Pitelis, 1998).

In all, the Marxist perspective considers the firm, the market and the state as complementary devices for the exploitation of the division of labour, but also the exploitation of labour (Pitelis, 1991). The emphasis is on sectional (capitalist) interests, not efficiency. The latter could be the outcome or the means but not the driving force. Put differently, efficiency could be sacrificed for the sake of sectional-class interests (Marglin, 1974).

From the discussion thus far, it could be suggested that there is an emerging consensus in economic theory to the effect that the three major institutions of capitalism discussed here should be seen partly as complements and partly as substitutes (Klein, Mahoney, McGahan, & Pitelis, 2010). The mutually exclusive focus on either efficiency or capitalist class interests, on the other hand, is, we think, far-fetched. Efficiency and sectional interests can often go hand in hand or be different sides of the same coin (Pitelis, 1991). Interestingly, 'neoclassical' economic historian North (1981) suggests that state functionaries will tend to pursue efficiency, only to the extent that their own interests are first maximized. This may point to some emerging consensus.

As we noted, the public choice and Chicago perspectives explicitly entertained the possibility of inefficiencies of state intervention (government failure), owing to opportunistic (or, more mildly, utility-maximizing) behaviour by state functionaries (bureaucrats, politicians) (Mueller, 2006). The maximization of state functionaries' utility and the demands by powerful organized groups of producers and trades unions which may capture the state helps explain, in this view, the state's growth in the Organisation for Economic Co-operation and Development countries (Mueller, 2006). From this perspective, in a well-functioning economy, markets should be left to operate freely, while the state should limit itself to the provision of stable rules of the game, for example, clear delineation of property rights.

### A Critical Synthesis and Extension and Its Implications for Sustainable Value Creation

The transaction cost and the public choice perspectives on the state have been brought together in North's (1981) attempt to provide a 'neoclassical' theory of the state. Here a wealth- or utility-maximizing ruler trades a group of services (e.g. protection, justice) for revenue, acting as a discriminating monopolist, by devising property rights for each, so as to maximize state revenue, subject to the constraint of potential entry into the territory controlled by other rulers (other states or parties). The objective is to maximize rents to the ruler and, subject to that, to reduce transaction costs in order to foster maximum output, and thus the tax revenues accruing to the ruler. The existing competition from rivals and the transaction costs in state activities typically tend to produce inefficient property rights: the former implies favouring powerful constituents, while transaction costs in metering, policing and collecting taxes provide incentives for states to grant monopolies. The existence of the two constraints gives rise to a conflict between a property rights structure that produces economic growth and one that maximizes rents to the ruler, and thus accounts for widespread inefficient property rights (Klein et al., 2013). North regarded this idea as the neoclassical variant of the Marxian notion of the contradictions in the mode of production, in which the ownership structure is incompatible with potential gains from existing technological opportunities (Pitelis, 1991).

There exist similarities between the public choice and North's view of the state and that of the Marxian School. Marx and his followers were among the first to contemplate a capture theory, which Marx, moreover, considered to be part and parcel of capitalism's existing inequalities in production (capitalists/workers). This inherent inequity, for Marx, implied a necessary bias of the state in favour of capitalists. This view has been elaborated by later-day Marxists, who pointed to instrumental reasons for this capitalist capture of the state, stressing either links of state personnel with capital and recruitment from unrepresentative elite backgrounds (Miliband, 1969) and/or structural reasons, such as control of capital over investments and the necessity to orchestrate relations between different fractions of capital (Poulantzas, 1969). Marxists explained the autonomous form of the capitalist state in terms of capital's direct control of labour in the production process (hence there was no need for the state to assume direct control of labour) and the need of the state to support production (provision of infrastructure, etc.) as a result of the anarchy of the market (the existence of many capitals: see Holloway & Picciotto, 1978). For the Marxist school, the growth of the state and fiscal crises can be explained in terms of the laws of motion of capitalism, such as the concentration and centralization of capital, declining profit rates and class struggle over the quantities of state expenditures and receipts (O'Connor, 1973).

Both North and the Marxist theories, however, underplay the power of consumers and what we prefer to call 'the polity' (the so-called 'third sector') at large, as electors and as a source of tax revenues. This in part is a result of their exclusive focus on economic determinism. The prospects of electoral defeat and reductions in the rents accruing to the state, resulting from reduced employment levels as a result of state policies, are constraints on the behaviour of state functionaries, whether they try to maximize their own utility or that of business. On the other hand, the possibility of capture is an important point of consensus between public choice and Marxian and North's theories. Moreover, it is not alien to the conventional neoclassical tradition (Krueger, 1974). Last but not least, the Marxian focus on the need to reduce production costs (already there in the conventional neoclassical focus on public goods, see Smith, 1776) counterbalances the exclusive reliance of transaction cost theorists on the exchange side.

The above summary of alternative perspectives on the possibility of capture allows a generalization of North's theory of the state. According to this, the state can be argued to exist because of excessive private sector transaction and production costs, and has as an objective to reduce these, so as to increase output and hence revenue for state functionaries. Increased output also helps to legitimize any income inequities. A constraint on the state's functionaries' attempt to achieve their objectives arises from the possibility of capture (inherent for Marxists, but arising ex-post for public choice theory). This tends to generate inefficient property rights, which in turn hinder increases in output. Transaction costs in metering, policing and enforcing taxes also lead to inefficiency in terms, for example, of states granting monopolies. Moreover, the cost of governing places a limit on the ability of the state to replace the private sector, leading to a need for a plurality of institutional forms (Mahoney, McGahan, & Pitelis, 2009; Pitelis, 1991).

It follows from the above that the aim of the state is, or should be, to reduce private sector transaction and production costs by removing the constraints which hinder the realization of appropriable value, such as the problem of capture by powerful constituents. This points towards the need to establish competitive conditions in product and labour markets. Competition in product and labour markets will tend to reduce but not eliminate constituent capture. It would, moreover, tend to reduce problems with governing costs associated, for example, with powerful opportunist private sector suppliers of requisite state services. Competitive conditions should not be limited to the private sector only but should be extended (to a lesser extent, so as not to facilitate capture and/or inefficiency due to discontinuities of state personnel) to the market for government control, so that politically mandated positions should also be up to a point contestable. This would provide useful sources of information on possible differences in the efficiency of governing.

The reduction of private and public sector transaction and production costs by the state is aimed at providing the conditions for the efficient production of goods and services by the economy, i.e. to increase supply side output and facilitate the realization of this output (its purchase by consumers, domestic or overseas). This helps introduce the concept of a national strategy for growth, as the set of state policies intended to reduce production and transaction costs so as to increase realized output in the form of income. The internalization of private sector activities by the state in this context should be pursued up to the point where an additional transaction or production activity would be produced at equal cost in the private sector (Pitelis, 1991). This could reinforce the concept of pluralism in institutional forms, i.e. the complementarity between the public and private sectors for the efficient production and allocation of resources (Klein et al., 2010; Stiglitz, 2000, 2011).

The notion of national strategy takes the revenue side as given, i.e. as the prerogative purely of the private sector. However, besides affecting production and transaction costs, a state can also affect the revenue side, if it consciously directs its production–transaction cost-reducing activities to particular areas and/or by directly undertaking production activities (Freeman, 2004; List, 1885). Such an attitude is particularly important in open economies with trade (Pasinetti, 2009; Pitelis, 2012b). In such a world, growth can be achieved via domestic and foreign demand, while income-rent will be affected positively through both reductions in transaction–production costs and increases in revenues through, for example, a focus on high-return sectors and/or the creation of agglomeration and clusters (Lin, 2011; Rodrik, 2009). It follows that national strategy could be designed to reduce overall production and transaction costs for the economy but also influence the revenue side, so as to increase the income accruing to the nation and hence taxes to the state. In this context state functionaries could be argued to act as public entrepreneurs (Klein et al., 2010). Such instances would also tend to endogenize the public–private nexus and require a theory of public entrepreneurship and its interaction with commercial entrepreneurship. Despite recent progress, economic theory is still far from such an analysis, which is more akin to political science, management and entrepreneurship scholarship (Klein et al., 2013).

Besides underplaying the issue of agency capable of changing the rules of the game (in the form of public and institutional entrepreneurship), the mainstream Marxist and neoclassical economics-based analyses so far are characterized by a degree of hyper-rationality, alien to organization and strategy scholars (Cyert & March, 1963; Nelson & Winter, 1982; Penrose, 1959). In real organizational life (Simon, 1995), uncertainty, limited and asymmetrical knowledge, sunk costs, learning, short-term versus long-term decision-making, history and path dependency as well as sheer incompetence can be important considerations. North's (2005) more recent work invokes the role of ideology in order to address the paradox of persisting inefficiency. However, ideology is also partly endogenous to the system of production, as dominant ideology tends to be aligned with those interests that have captured the state – the classic case being Thatcherism and the growth of monetarism and financialization. Dominant ideologies tend to be more in line with the views represented by the ruling elites (Argitis & Pitelis, 2001). Marxist-inspired theories would see ideological differences being reflective of structural interests: it is these and how they are represented that help explain why particular ideologies should exist or emerge that in some cases foster while in others hinder institutional change, that, for instance, places systemic efficiency above non-efficiency, or vice versa, as when producer groups gain tariff protection or when labour restricts open immigration into the national labour market.

A novel perspective on this crucial question should leverage organization and strategy scholarship, notably capabilities and evolutionary ideas (Klein et al., 2013). For example, it is arguable that efficiency-promoting institutional change will tend to dominate when rulers have developed capabilities to build a 'value capture model' that allows them to maintain and enhance inter-temporally their privileged positions. If the context was one of certainty and unlimited rationality, rulers could always choose the action that maximizes the net present value of wealth accrued. With uncertainty, limited rationality and learning, the critical issue becomes how to acquire the highest possible net present value. The mechanism could involve instituting a 'value capture model-power structure' that affords continuing inter-temporal accrual of wealth of a constant or increasing stream of returns, from an existing pool (or even a decreasing share from an expanding pool provided that the reduced share still affords higher returns), subject to minimizing the risks of expropriation, ostracism and/or exclusion. In real life, this involves setting up structures, organizations, institutions and developing requisite capabilities that make the desired outcome more likely (Klein, Mahoney, McGahan, & Pitelis, 2012b; Pitelis & Teece, 2010). Arguably, when rulers feel confident enough that they have engendered a set-up that, more or less, guarantees increased viability and legitimacy, alongside increased returns (even and especially when these are a declining ratio of the total) then, subject to learning curves and capabilities, they would tend to favour institutional changes that foster efficiency because their 'value capture model' will allow them to keep receiving desired benefits and an expanding (through enhanced efficiency) surplus. In contrast, when the value capture model is weak or precarious, rulers will devote resources to building up and strengthening value capture capabilities, even at the expense of efficiency (North, 1990). In all cases, an essential pre-condition is to minimize free riding on the part of members of the ruling elite (Olson, 1965).

Historically, the two-party system in advanced capitalist countries has functioned as a value capture model for the rulers of both parties and proved itself capable of delivering the goods for a period of time. 'Rival' rulers rule, on average, for comparable periods, during which each receives a disproportionate share of the spoils. However, for a complex set of reasons (such as the eventual dissatisfaction of the electorate), it is almost certain that the roles will be reversed. The opposition party can serve as consultants in the private sector, set up non-profit organizations subsidized by the 'state' to keep paying fat salaries to their clientele and sometimes themselves, etc. Importantly, political parties develop ways to reduce free riding. These involve keeping access to relational positions that offer opportunities for the exercise of power, developing new capacities to inflict mutual damage, keeping hostages to facilitate exchange and, overall, using sticks and carrots that make defection too expensive. These characteristics partly address the free-rider problem. Within limits, such systems seem to work best for rulers, while also fostering efficiency. It would appear that countries that adopt this system, through a process of learning by their rulers, perform best in terms of efficiency. Besides reducing the risks we alluded to the added advantage of such a system is that it offers legitimacy through external comparisons that can, in turn, help internal politics.

It is not always possible, however, to establish a value capture apparatus and deal with free riding. Learning curves and competencies aside, this is because in some countries' history, initial conditions, external threats, wars, religious and ideological fractions, and the continued threat of exclusion, ostracism and expropriation make unavailable the internal and external conditions that are necessary and sufficient for value capture by the rulers and sustainable system-wide value creation to be aligned. In some cases the rulers are themselves the leading free riders. In the real world of organizations' strategies, conflicting interests and power structures, the conditions for efficiency and power relations to be simultaneously observed are rather tight. This can help explain the prevalence of inefficient private – public structures (Klein et al., 2012b). Bringing into the analysis the aforementioned real-life traits is critical. However, this requires going far beyond organizational economics, towards a multi-and cross-disciplinary perspective that brings in organization theory strategy and entrepreneurship.

For the purposes of this paper suffice it to say that the current crisis, and importantly the response to it by the ruling elites, portrays a clear regression from value enhancing to value redistributing and indeed destroying policies (Pitelis, 2012a). In a real sense we are observing applied Marxism, in that the needs for restructuring, power consolidation and sectional interests outweigh any interests in sustainable value creation. We are witnessing policies that destroy future sources of growth, such as the environment and the future generations. If anything, countries that have been moving for years towards the value-creation-given distribution route are now regressing towards sectional interest promotion and even plutocracy (Zingales, 2012). Keynes' clarion call to save capitalism from capitalists becomes more relevant than ever. Hayek (1944), the alleged father figure of neoliberalism, sounds radical, even revolutionary, in his own clarion call to foster competition, not business (interests). Extant theories from economics on the public – private nexus hardly touch upon even the surface of such issues. We need a social science-based integrated theory of organizational, economic and social change and stability. To this end strategy can be of import, but so do sociology and political science, history and entrepreneurship.

## Conclusion

Organizational economic theories of private (business, industry) and public organization draw on alternative perspectives. Dominant among these is that of market failure, albeit in more recent years evolutionary, knowledge, DCs and systems-based views have been making significant inroads – especially on the theory of the firm, public policy and business strategy.

Our critical account of the extensive literature pointed to commonalities and remaining differences and attempted a synthesis and extension. Our extension leveraged ideas from evolutionary theory and business strategy and examined their implications for enhancing system-wide efficiency and sustainable value creation through requisite public – private mixes. The analysis highlighted the difficulties associated with establishing a socioeconomic structure that fosters sustainable value creation. This helps explain the persistence of inefficiency and in part the current regression of countries that were previously seen as exemplars, towards sectional interests and even plutocracy.

In addition to the above, we pointed to limitations of extant theory and our synthesis, not least in terms of the need for an agency-based perspective that recognizes entrepreneurship, private and public, as well as real-life conditions of uncertainty, procedural and limited rationality, conflict and learning. While we introduced some elements of such an approach, clearly more needs to be done in this direction. This necessitates an integrated multi- and cross-disciplinary analysis that also leverages sociology and political science. We intend to pursue such an approach in future research and hope that other scholars will be motivated to do so.

## References

Alchian, A., & Demsetz, H. (1972). Production, information costs and economic organization. *American Economic Review, 62*(5), 777–795.

Argitis, G., & Pitelis, C. (2001). Monetary policy and the distribution of income: Evidence for the United States and the United Kingdom. *Journal of Post Keynesian Economics, 23*(4), 617–638.

Arrow, K. J. (1970). The organization of economic activity: Issues pertinent to the choice of market versus non-market allocation. In R. Haveman & J. Margolis (Eds.), *Public expenditure and policy analysis* (pp. 59–73). Chicago, IL: Markham.

Barney, J. B. (1991). Firm resources and sustained competitive advantage. *Journal of Management, 17*(1), 99–120.

Barney, J. B. (2001). Resource-based theories of competitive advantage: A ten-year retrospective on the resource-based view. *Journal of Management, 27*(6), 643–650.

Baumol, W. J. (1991). *Perfect markets and easy virtue – Business ethics and the invisible hand.* Cambridge, MA: Blackwell.

Berle, A. A., & Means, G. C. (1932). *The modern corporation and private property.* New York, NY: Commerce Clearing House.

Clegg, S. R., Boreham, P., & Dow, G. (1986). *Class, politics and the economy.* London/Boston, MA: Routledge and Kegan Paul/The International Library of Sociology.

Coase, R. H. (1937). The nature of the firm. *Economica, 4*, 386–405.

Coase, R. H. (1960). The problem of social cost. *Journal of Law and Economics, 3*, 1–44.

Coase, R. H. (1991). The nature of the firm: Influence. In O. E. Williamson & S. G. Winter (Eds.), *The nature of the firm: Origins, evolution and development* (pp. 61–74). Oxford: Oxford University Press.

Cohen, M. D., March, J. G., & Olsen, J. P. (1972). The garbage can model of organizational choice. *Administrative Science Quarterly, 17*(1), 1–25.

Cohen, R. B., Felton, N., Van Liere, J., & Nikosi, M. (Eds.). (1979). *The multinational corporation: A radical approach, papers by Stephen Herbert Hymer.* Cambridge: Cambridge University Press.

Cyert, R. M., & March, J. G. (1963). *A behavioural theory of the firm.* Cliffs, NJ: Englewood Prentice Hall.

David, R. J., & Han, S. (2004). A systematic assessment of the empirical support for transaction cost economics. *Strategic Management Journal, 25*, 39–58.

Demsetz, H. (1973). Industry structure, market rivalry, and public policy. *Journal of Law and Economics, 16*, 1–9.

Demsetz, H. (1988). The theory of the firm revisited. *Journal of Law, Economics, and Organization, 4*(1), 141–162.

Edquist, C. (2005). Systems of innovation: Perspectives and challenges. In F. Fagerberg, D. C. Mowery & R. R. Nelson (Eds.), *The Oxford handbook of innovation* (pp. 181–208). Oxford: Oxford University Press.

Eggertsson, T. (1990). *Economic behaviour and institutions.* Cambridge: Cambridge University Press.

Eisenhardt, K. M., & Martin, J. A. (2000). Dynamic capabilities: What are they? *Strategic Management Journal, 21*, 1105–1121.

Freeman, C. (2004). Technological infrastructure and international competitiveness. *Industrial and Corporate Change, 13*(3), 541–569.

Friedman, M. (1962). *Capitalism and freedom*. Chicago, IL: University of Chicago Press.

Gilbert, R. J., & Newbery, D. M. G. (1982). Preemptive patenting and the persistence of monopoly. *American Economic Review*, *72*(2), 514–526.

Grossman, S. J., & Hart, O. (1986). The costs and benefits of ownership: A theory of vertical and lateral integration. *Journal of Political Economy*, *94*(4), 691–718.

Hall, P. A., & Soskice, D. (2001). *Varieties of capitalism: The institutional foundations of comparative advantage*. New York, NY: Oxford University Press.

Harcourt, G. C., & Kriesler, P. (2012). "Introduction" (*To handbook of post-Keynesian economics: Oxford University Press, USA*) (May 3, 2012). (UNSW Australian School of Business Research Paper No. 2012–33). Available at SSRN: Retrieved from http://ssrn.com/abstract=2064239

Hardin, R. (1997). Economic theories of the state. In D. Mueller (Ed.), *Perspectives on public choice: A handbook* (pp. 21–34). Cambridge: Cambridge University Press.

Hart, O. (1995). *Firms, contracts, and financial structure*. Oxford: Clarendon.

Hay, C., Lister, M., & Marsh, D. (Eds.) (2006). *The state: Theories and issues*. Basingstoke: Macmillan.

Hayek, F. (1944). *The road to serfdom*. Chicago, IL: University of Chicago Press.

Hayek, F. (1945). The use of knowledge in society. *The American Economic Review*, *35*, 519–530.

Helfat, C., Finkelstein, S., Mitchell, W., Peteraf, M. A., Singh, H., Teece, D. J., & Winter, S. G. (2007). *Dynamic capabilities: Understanding strategic change in organizations*. Oxford: Blackwell.

Helfat, C. E., & Winter, S. G. (2011). Untangling dynamic and operational capabilities: Strategy for the (N)ever-changing world. *Strategic Management Journal*, *32*, 1243–1250.

Holloway, J., & Picciotto, S. (1978). *State and capital: A Marxist debate*. London: Edward Arnold.

Hunt, S. D. (2000). *A general theory of competition: Resources, competences, productivity, economic growth*. Thousand Oaks, CA: Sage Publications.

Jensen, M. C., & Meckling, W. H. (1976). Theory of the firm: Managerial behaviour, agency costs and ownership structure. *Journal of Financial Economics*, *3*(4), 304–360.

Katkalo, V. S., Pitelis, C. N., & Teece, D. J. (2010). Introduction: On the nature and scope of dynamic capabilities. *Industrial and Corporate Change*, *19*, 1175–1186.

Kim, J., & Mahoney, J. T. (2002). Resource-based and property rights perspectives on value creation: The case of oil field unitization. *Managerial and Decision Economics*, *23*(4), 225–245.

Klein, P. G., Mahoney, J. T., McGahan, A. M., & Pitelis, C. N. (2010). Toward a theory of public entrepreneurship. *European Management Review*, *7*, 1–15.

Klein, P. G., Mahoney, J. T., McGahan, A. M., & Pitelis, C. N. (2012a). Who is in charge? A property rights perspective on stakeholder governance. *SO! APBOX Special Issue*, *10*(3), 304–315.

Klein, P. G., Mahoney, J. T., McGahan, A. M., & Pitelis, C. N. (2012b). *Governance, innovation and sustainable competitive advantage: The co-adaptation of organizations and institutions*. Mimeo.

Klein, P. G., Mahoney, J. T., McGahan, A. M., & Pitelis, C. N. (2013). Capabilities and strategic entrepreneurship in public organizations. *Strategic Entrepreneurship Journal*, *7*(1), 70–91.

Krueger, A. O. (1974). The political economy of the rent-seeking society. *American Economic Review*, *64*, 291–303.

Lazonick, W., & O'Sullivan, M. (2000). Maximizing shareholder value: A new ideology for corporate governance. *Economy and Society*, *29*(1), 13–35.

Lin, J. Y. (2011). *Demystifying the Chinese economy*. Cambridge: Cambridge University Press.

Lippman, S. A., & Rumelt, R. (2003). The payments perspective: Micro-foundations of resource analysis. *Strategic Management Journal*, *24*, 903–927.

List, F. (1885). *The national system of political economy*. London: Longmans Green.

Lundvall, B. Å. (2007). National innovation systems – Analytical concept and development tool. *Industry and Innovation*, *14*(1), 95–119.

Mahoney, J. T., McGahan, A. M., & Pitelis, C. N. (2009). The interdependence of private and public interests. *Organization Science*, *20*(6), 1034–1052.

Mahoney, J. T., & Pandian, R. J. (1992). The resource-based view within the conversation of strategic management. *Strategic Management Journal*, *13*(5), 363–380.

March, J. G., & Simon, H. A. (1958). *Organizations*. New York, NY: Wiley.

Marglin, S. (1974). What do bosses do? The origins and functions of hierarchy in capitalist production. *Review of Radical Political Economics*, *6*, 60–112.

Marris, R. (1996). Managerial theories of the firm. In M. Warner (Ed.), *International encyclopaedia of business and management* (pp. 3117–3125). London: Routledge.

Marshall, A. (1920). *Principles of economics*. London: Macmillan.

Marx, K. (1959). *Capital*. London: Lawrence and Wishart.

Miliband, R. (1969). *The state in capitalist society*. London: Quarter Books.

Mueller, D. C. (2006). Corporate governance and economic performance. *International Review of Applied Economics, 20*(5), 623–643.

Nelson, R. R., & Winter, S. G. (1982). *An evolutionary theory of economic change*. Cambridge, MA: Belknap/Harvard University Press.

North, D. C. (1981). *Structure and change in economic history*. New York, NY: Norton.

North, D. C. (1990). *Institutions, institutional change and economic performance*. Cambridge: Cambridge University Press.

North, D. C. (2005). *Understanding the process of economic change*. Princeton, NJ: Princeton University Press.

O'Connor, J. (1973). *The fiscal crisis of the state*. New York, NY: St Martin's Press.

Olson, M. (1965). *The logic of collective action: Public goods and the theory of groups*. Cambridge, MA: Harvard University Press.

Ostrom, E. (2011). Reflections on "Some Unsettled Problems of Irrigation". *American Economic Review, 101*, 49–63.

Pasinetti, L. (2009). *Keynes and the Cambridge Keynesians: A 'Revolution in Economics' to be accomplished*. Cambridge: Cambridge University Press.

Penrose, E. T. (1959). *The theory of the growth of the firm*. Oxford: Oxford University Press.

Pepall, L., Richards, D. J., & Norman, G. (2008). *Industrial organization: Contemporary theory and empirical applications*. Wiley-Blackwell.

Peteraf, M. (1993). The cornerstone of competitive advantage. *Strategic Management Journal, 14*, 179–191.

Peteraf, M., & Barney, J. B. (2003). Unravelling the resource based Tangle. *Managerial and Decision Economics, 24*(4), 309–323.

Pitelis, C. N. (1991). *Market and non-market hierarchies: Theory of institutional failure*. Oxford: Basil Blackwell Publishing.

Pitelis, C. N. (1998). Transaction costs and the historical evolution of the capitalist firm. *Journal of Economic Issues, 32*(4), 999–1017.

Pitelis, C. N. (2002). *The growth of the firm: The legacy of Edith Penrose*. Oxford: Oxford University Press.

Pitelis, C. N. (2007). A behavioral resource-based view of the firm – The synergy of Cyert and March (1963) and Penrose (1959). *Organization Science, 18*(3), 337–349.

Pitelis, C. N. (2009a). The sustainable competitive advantage and catching-up of nations: FDI, clusters and liability (asset) of smallness. *Management International Review, 49*, 95–120.

Pitelis, C. N. (2009b). The co-evolution of organizational value capture, value creation and sustainable advantage. *Organization Studies, 30*(10), 1115–1139.

Pitelis, C. N. (2012a). On PIIGS, GAFFs, and BRICs: An insider–outsider perspective on structural and institutional foundations of the Greek crisis. *Contributions to Political Economy, 31*(1), 77–89.

Pitelis, C. N. (2012b, September 12–13). *Innovation, resource creation, learning and catching-up: Building on Pasinetti to Revitalize Cambridge Economics*. Paper presented at "The economics of structural change: Theory, institutions and policy, a conference in honour of Luigi L. Pasinetti", Cambridge.

Pitelis, C. N. (2012c). Clusters, entrepreneurial ecosystem co-creation, and appropriability: A conceptual framework. *Industrial and Corporate Change, 21*(6), 1359–1388.

Pitelis, C. N., & Clarke, T. (1993). Introduction: The political economy of privatization. In T. Clarke & C. Pitelis (Eds.), *The political economy of privatization* (pp. 1–28). London: Routledge.

Pitelis, C. N., & Teece, D. J. (2009). The (New) nature and essence of the firm. *European Management Review, 6*(1), 5–15.

Pitelis, C. N., & Teece, D. J. (2010). Cross-border market co-creation, dynamic capabilities and the entrepreneurial theory of the multinational enterprise. *Industrial and Corporate Change, 19*(4), 1–37.

Porter, M. E. (1990). *The competitive advantage of nations*. Basingstoke: Macmillan.

Porter, M. E. (1991). Towards a dynamic theory of strategy. *Strategic Management Journal, 12*, 95–117.

Poulantzas, N. (1969). *Political power and social class*. London: New Left Books.

Pressman, S. (2006). *Alternative theories of the state*. Basingstoke: Palgrave Macmillan.

Priem, R. L., & Butler, J. E. (2001). Is the resource-based theory a useful perspective for strategic management research? *Academy of Management Review, 26*(1), 22–40.

Pusey, M. (1991). *Economic rationalism in Canberra: A nation-building state changes its mind*. Cambridge: Cambridge University Press.

Richardson, G. B. (1972). The organisation of industry. *Economic Journal, 82*, 883–896.

Rodrik, D. (2009). The new development economics: We shall experiment, but how shall we learn? In J. Cohen & W. Easterly (Eds.), *What works in development? Thinking big and thinking small* (pp. 24–54). Washington, DC: Brookings Institution Press.

Schumpeter, J. (1942). *Capitalism, socialism and democracy* (5th ed.). London: Unwin Hyman (1987).

Simon, H. (1947). *Administrative behavior.* New York, NY: The Free Press.

Simon, H. (1955). A behavioral model of rational choice. *Quarterly Journal of Economics, 69*(1), 99–118.

Simon, H. (1995). Organizations and markets. *Journal of Public Administration Research & Theory, 5*(3), 273–295.

Smith, A. (1776). *An enquiry into the nature and causes of the wealth of nations. The Glasgow edition of the works and correspondence of Adam Smith.* London: Strahan & Cadell.

Starbuck, W. (1983). Organizations as action generators. *American Sociological Review, 48*, 91–102.

Stigler, G. (1988). The effect of government on economic efficiency. *Business Economics, 23*, 7–13.

Stiglitz, J. (2000). *Economics of the public sector* (3rd ed.). W.W. Norton & Company.

Stiglitz, J. (2011). Rethinking development economics. *The World Bank Research Observer, 26*, 230–236.

Teece, D. J. (1982). Towards an economic theory of the multiproduct firm. *Journal of Economic Behavior and Organization, 3*(1), 39–63.

Teece, D. J. (2007). Explicating dynamic capabilities: The nature and microfoundations of (Sustainable) enterprise performance. *Strategic Management Journal, 28*(13), 1319–1350.

Teece, D. J., Pisano, G., & Shuen, A. (1997). Dynamic capabilities and strategic management. *Strategic Management Journal, 18*(7), 509–533.

Tirole, J. (1988). *The theory of industrial organization.* MIT Press Books.

Weber, M. (1947). *The theory of social and economic organization.* New York, NY: Free Press.

Wernerfelt, B. (1984). The resource-based view of the firm. *Strategic Management Journal, 5*, 171–180.

Wignaraja, G. (Ed.) (2003). *Competitiveness strategy and industrial performance in developing countries: A manual policy analysis.* Routledge.

Williamson, O. E. (1975). *Markets and Hierarchies: Analysis and antitrust implications. A study in the economics of internal organization.* New York, NY: The Free Press.

Williamson, O. E. (1985). *The economic institutions of capitalism.* New York, NY: Free Press.

Williamson, O. E. (1991). Strategizing, economizing, and economic organization. *Strategic Management Journal, 12*, 75–94.

Winter, S. G. (2012, October 11). *Pursuing the evolutionary agenda in economics and management research: Reflections at the 30th anniversary of Nelson & Winter.* Presented at the conference on dynamic capabilities and the sustainable competitiveness of firms and nations, St. Petersburg, Russia.

Wolf, C., Jr. (1979). A theory of non-market failure: Framework for implementation analysis. *Journal of Law and Economics, 22*(1), 107–140.

Zingales, L. (2012). *A capitalism for the people: Recapturing the Lost Genius of American prosperity.* New York, NY: Basic Books.

# The 'Why Not'–Perspective of Green Purchasing: A Multilevel Case Study Analysis

EDELTRAUD GUENTHER, ANNE-KAREN HUESKE, KRISTIN STECHEMESSER & LIOBA BUSCHER

*Technische Universitaet Dresden/Faculty of Business and Economics, Dresden, Germany*

ABSTRACT *To support organizations in their greening efforts the normative and instrumental 'how to' perspective is indispensable. However, the descriptive 'why not' perspective adds valuable insights to factors that may hamper, decelerate or even block green purchasing. Our study follows Eisenhardt's design for case study research and comprises three stages: in the first stage, we analysed barriers to green procurement in six municipalities in five European countries; in the second stage, we combined those findings with the literature on multilevel research, present a barrier framework based on a multilevel categorization and develop hypotheses by analysing the organizational and the individual level in one of the biggest procurement agencies in Europe. In the third stage, we test the derived hypotheses and draw conclusions. In order to be able to deeply analyse one specific decision process and its inherent barriers we focused on the procurement process due to its gatekeeper position in organizations. We contribute to understanding the greening of organizations via the 'why not' perspective by answering the question 'Why do organizations not implement green purchasing?' As organizations are multilevel systems, this paper illustrates how the differentiation of the multiple levels of analysis and the detailed analysis of one specific task can contribute to understand greening organizations and moreover to continuously improve greening in organizations. Our study is designed as a multilevel analysis examining the relationships between the individual, group, organizational level, and the external environment that lead to barriers for green purchasing. The multilevel framework can be used for analysing barriers in green purchasing. Complementing the 'how to' perspective with taking the 'why not perspective' we look on the challenges managers, who foster sustainability, are confronted with.*

## Introduction

Organizations have been claimed responsible for their role in society (McWilliams & Siegel, 2000) and their impacts upon the environment (Hart, 1995; Henriques & Sadorsky, 1999). Consequently, different approaches for greening organizations have been developed over the last 30 years (Brief & Motowidlo, 1986; Boiral, 2009; Daily, Bishop, & Govindarajulu, 2009). In this paper we focus on procurement as it plays a strategic role for greening organizations (Bala, Munoz, Rieradevall, & Ysern, 2008; Murray, 2000; Walker, Di Sisto, & McBain, 2008). As a crucial activity within organizations (Murray, 2000), procurement holds a gatekeeper position in greening the organization as it is linked with all departments (Guenther, Greschner Farkavcová, & Scheibe, 2010). Especially in the public sector, which is often more focused on supply of services instead of manufacturing of goods, greening procurement is a vital step towards fostering green management (Cunningham & Kempling, 2009).

Although all members of the Organisation for Economic Co-operation and Development (OECD) have committed to encourage green purchasing in their administration on the national, regional, and local level (Ochoa & Erdmenger, 2003) and many studies focused on the normative and instrumental 'how to' perspective, i.e. the question how organizations can enhance their initiatives for the environment (Brief & Motowidlo, 1986; Boiral, 2009; Daily et al., 2009). But the greening of organizations is not yet mainstream as barriers still prevail (Ren, 2009; Thun & Müller, 2010; Wirtz, Lutje, & Schierz, 2010) and greening efforts often fail to be integrated and implemented in day-to-day business decisions in organizations. The insight that the mere 'how to implement greening' perspective is necessary, but not sufficient, raises the question: 'Why do organizations fail to implement greening?' or more specifically 'What are the barriers to greening procurement in public sector organizations?' There exists a multitude of answers, which name factors, so-called barriers, which may hamper, decelerate, or even block greening efforts in organizations. When conducting a literature review we found studies that revealed lists of barriers, but no comprehensive framework. Brander and Olsthoorn (2002) conducted interviews and a questionnaire-based survey among the European Buy-it-Green-Network and finally provided a list of barriers including the availability of green alternatives, the availability of information, and the transparency of legal rules. They identified political commitment and procurement officers to be considered as a major source for barriers. Ochoa and Erdmenger (2003) conducted a survey among 4,000 procurement officials in Europe and ended up with the barrier categories lack of interest, lack of money, and lack of environmental knowledge and concerns about the legal rules. Guenther and Scheibe (2005) analysed barriers for green procurement in European municipalities and identified the barriers no aim, no regulations, no information, no knowledge, and no incentive and sanction system. The Parliament House of Commons Environment Audit Committee (EAC) (2005) analysed the procurement behaviour in the UK via workshops and categorized the barriers into two groups: in the first group they integrated lack of leadership, lack of definitions and measurements, lack of incentive systems, and lack of learning from the field; to the second group belonged lack of accountability, short-termism, lack of leadership, and lack of clear policy. Brammer and Walker (2007) analysed barriers for procurement by conducting a survey among 280 procurement practitioners worldwide and grouped the barriers into financial, informational, legal, managerial, political, quality, and priority barriers. Defranceschi and Hidson (2007) interviewed individuals in the public sector in the UK and identified the lack of leadership, the culture of public sector procurement, the failure to deliver on agreed action and approaches, the lack of competence, structural complications, the perception of cost, and the complexity of the process as barrier groups. Løland Dolva (2007) analysed public procurement in Norway via qualitative interviews and presented five barrier groups: knowledge, cost, lack of support and focus, focus on functionality, and work pressure. The OECD (2007) conducted a survey in 19 OECD countries and came up with the major barriers of lack of training, lack of practical tools, fear of non-compliance, motivation, time, knowledge, and distrust of new products. Steurer, Berger, Konrad, and Martinuzzi (2007) analysed barriers for procurement in 26 European countries by interviewing those responsible for the procurement initiatives and identified the barriers of time pressure, lack of training, complexity of processes, short-term budgeting, insufficient support, and lack of resources. Walker and Brammer (2007) conducted a survey among 106 procurement officers in the UK and identified the barriers of conflicting priorities, lack of long-term view, time pressure, lack of guidance, lack of pressure, conflicting objectives, and fear of change. Geng and Doberstein (2008) conducted a case study in the Chinese governmental sector and identified the lack of necessary guidelines, the inconsistent use of indicators, gaps in the existing environmental legal system, decisions based on costs only, and the low environmental awareness of both procurers and suppliers as barriers. Hanks, Davies, and Perera (2008) interviewed senior officials in municipalities in South Africa and categorized the barriers as financial, market-related, institutional, equity-related, and system-related. Walker et al. (2008) interviewed public and private procurers in seven organizations in the UK and presented the internal barriers of costs and lack of legitimacy and the external barriers of regulation, poor supplier commitment, and industry-specific barriers. To conclude, we could identify lists of barriers, but no comprehensive framework of even barrier theory. Consequently, our study comprises three stages of analysis following the eight steps of Eisenhardt (1989): getting started, selecting cases, crafting instruments and protocols, entering the field, analysing data, shaping hypotheses, enfolding literature, and reaching closure: the first stage comprises the steps 1–5 of Eisenhardt (1989), where we analysed barriers to green procurement in six municipalities in five European countries; in the second stage corresponding to steps 6 and 7 of Eisenhardt (1989), we combine those findings with the literature on multilevel research, present a barrier framework based on a multilevel categorization and develop hypotheses by analysing the organizational and the individual level in one of the biggest procurement agencies in Europe. In the third stage (step 8 of Eisenhardt, 1989) we test the derived hypotheses and draw conclusions.

We contribute to the understanding of the greening of organizations via the 'why not' perspective by answering the question 'Why do organizations not implement green purchasing?' As organizations are multilevel systems (Klein & Kozlowski, 2000b), this paper will illustrate how the differentiation of the multiple levels of analysis and the detailed analysis of one specific task can contribute to an understanding of greening organizations and, moreover, to continuously improve greening in organizations.

**Stage 1: missing barrier theory as starting point for case study research**

An analysis of studies on barriers to greening organizations showed there is no existing barrier theory that could be applied for testing hypotheses (Bala et al., 2008; Guenther & Scheibe, 2005; Post & Altman, 1994; Thun & Müller, 2010). Therefore, we chose to follow the eight steps of Eisenhardt, as it is appropriate for exploring a phenomenon that lacks theoretical explanation (Eisenhardt, 1989). In step 1, *getting started*, we chose a multiple case method due to the complex nature of the phenomenon as well as to allow the investigation of multi-dimensional issues within the particular context and, as such, richer theory can be generated with multiple case studies than with a single case (Eisenhardt, 1989); the multiple case study was designed based on the suitability of this qualitative approach (Yin, 2003).

In step 2, *selecting cases*, we followed the concept of theoretical sampling (Eisenhardt, 1989) and selected six municipalities with varying size (50,000 to 1.7 million inhabitants), experience with greening (1 up to 16 years), and legal background (members and non-member of the European Union, and from different European countries) (Table 1). Moreover, a case study analysis of several public authorities allowed inter-organizational comparisons.

In step 3, *crafting instruments and protocols*, we consulted a European expert panel to identify the best-suited data collection methods and informants. To reach triangulation of evidence, multiple data collection methods were applied (Eisenhardt, 1989): expert interviews, content analysis of archival data, and structured questionnaires. The interview guidelines were developed in cooperation with an expert panel. Two investigators (the first author and another member of the research team) conducted the interviews. Notes were taken and analysed by two members of the research team.

In step 4, *entering the field*, we conducted semi-structured interviews to identify innovation barriers, starting in the first round with the heads of procurement, in order to define individuals and groups involved in decision-making that could give insights into possible barriers. In order to not rely on the perspective of one individual, the interviewees could co-nominate other individuals following

**Table 1.** Case characteristics.

| Case | Country | Size (in inhabitants) | Experience in greening (in years) |
|---|---|---|---|
| A | Germany | 1,700,000 | 5 |
| B | Germany | 590,000 | 16 |
| C | Sweden | 260,000 | 6 |
| D | Denmark | 50,000 | 7 |
| E | Switzerland | 360,000 | 14 |
| F | Hungary | 180,000 | 1 |

the opportunistic data collection method in order to 'take advantage of emergent themes' (Eisenhardt, 1989, p. 533). Merging the results of all municipalities, the typical organization could be split into a strategic level, comprising the head of the municipality and the responsible politician, and an operational level, consisting of the procurement department, the finance department, the environmental department, and the user belonging to any department within the municipality authority. Depending on the size of the municipality, the departments themselves were structured with a strategic and an operational level. The main external institutions mentioned by the interviewees having an influence on barriers for greening procurement were the state (legal environment), by its fiscal and non-fiscal instruments; the market (economic environment), by delivering green alternatives; and the citizens (societal environment), by representing the awareness for greening in the society and revealing their attitude during elections.

We consequently selected the individuals on the strategic and the operational level from the identified groups (Figure 1) for interviews in the second round. Overall we interviewed 49 individuals ranging from three individuals in a small municipality with 60,000 inhabitants to 12 individuals in a large city with 1.7 million inhabitants. The aim of those interviews was to undertake a rough screening to get an overview on the perception of barriers of different individuals involved in procurement decisions and working on different organizational levels.

The interviews were complemented with archival data analysis of procurement guidelines, reports, and studies with the aim to assess the penetration of environmental management in the municipality. In addition, multiple investigators and informants ensured the inclusion of divergent perspectives. Finally, 22 barriers were identified (Table 2).

In the third round we extended the method by transferring these barriers into a four-level Likert scale questionnaire, ranging from 'I agree that ... is a barrier' to

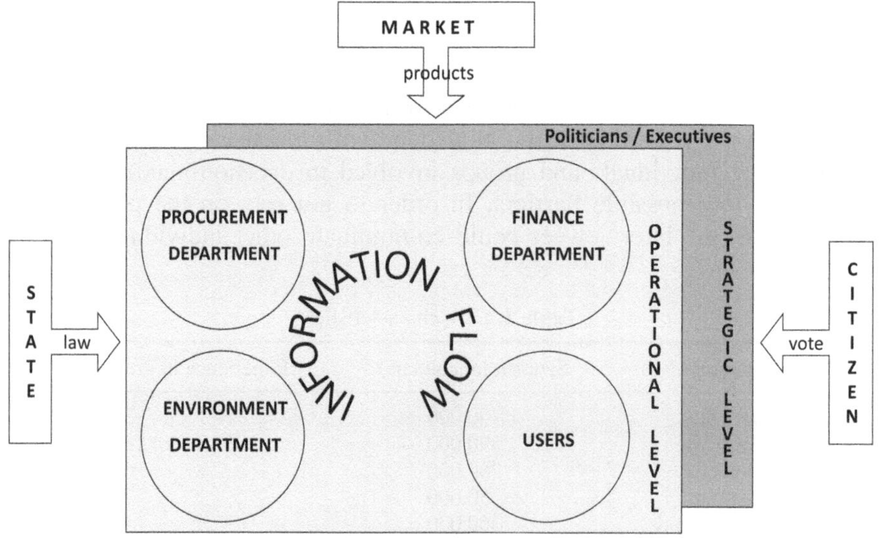


**Figure 1.** Actor model.

**Table 2.** Barriers catalogue.

| | Barrier statement | Shortened form |
|---|---|---|
| 1 | Efforts for the further implementation of green procurement are useful (barrier, if not supported) | Efforts not useful |
| 2 | Green procurement is one of the aims of my municipality/organization (barrier, if not supported) | No aim (of my organization) |
| 3 | There are different views at several decision levels of my local authority concerning the inclusion of environmental criteria in the field of public procurement | Different views |
| 4 | I am sufficiently informed about the aim of green procurement (barrier, if not supported) | Not informed about aim |
| 5 | I am informed about the possibilities of green procurement (barrier, if not supported) | Not informed about possibilities |
| 6 | Initiatives of employees who want to procure green are supported (barrier, if not supported) | Initiatives not encouraged |
| 7 | Existing procurement guidelines do support the inclusion of environmental criteria in procurement decisions in a sufficient way (barrier, if not supported) | Guidelines do not support |
| 8 | Given possibilities to include environmental criteria are widely used in my municipality (barrier, if not supported) | Possibilities not widely used |
| 9 | There are uncertainties concerning the legal position of green procurement (e.g. because of complexity) | Uncertain legal position |
| 10 | The applicable law concerning the inclusion of environmental criteria is very complex | Law very complex |
| 11 | The existing legal framework supports green procurement (barrier, if not supported) | Legal framework prevents |
| 12 | I am informed about the environmental relevance of procured product and service alternatives (barrier, if not supported) | Not informed about relevance |
| 13 | Information (criteria, prices, services) concerning green product and service alternatives is available (barrier, if not supported) | Missing information about alternatives |
| 14 | It is difficult to identify green product and service alternatives within the procurement market | Difficult to identify |
| 15 | There are sufficient green product and service alternatives available within the procurement market (barrier, if not supported) | No green alternatives available |
| 16 | Environmentally friendly products and services are too expensive | Too expensive |
| 17 | Green products and services have a lower functionality compared to conventional products | Lower functionality |
| 18 | Many users have prejudices concerning environmentally friendly product and services alternatives | User prejudice |
| 19 | Green procurement is obstructed by the administration processes (e.g. due to spread competences) | Administration process hurdle |
| 20 | Green procurement causes additional work | Additional work |
| 21 | Follow-up costs (e.g. energy and disposal costs) are not included in procurement decisions | Follow-up costs not included |
| 22 | Higher demand for environmentally friendly product and services alternatives by users within the municipality is a premise for more environmental procurement | Higher demand prerequisite |

'I do not agree that ... is a barrier', and used it for structured interviews. Besides the aim of assessing the perceived relevance of potential barriers, we asked for the function of the interview partner, i.e. his or her perceived influence to implement green procurement. This allowed us to conduct with-in case analyses and to identify any cross case pattern (Eisenhardt, 1989).

Thereafter we *analysed the data* in step 5 of Eisenhardt's framework by interpreting the differences in perception between the individuals and groups. Interestingly enough, for all barriers except three (Table 3), the answers over all 49 individuals ranged from 'I agree that ... is a barrier' (which is represented by 4) to 'I do not agree that ... is a barrier' (which is represented by 1). The three answers 'Efforts for the further implementation of green procurement are useful (barrier, if not supported)' (shortened form: 'efforts not useful'), 'Green procurement is one of the aims of my municipality (barrier, if not supported)' (shortened form: 'no aim'), and 'I am sufficiently informed about the aim of green procurement (barrier, if not supported)' (shortened form: 'not informed about the aim') were the only answers where no individual saw a definite barrier. This indicates that they were all aware of the participation of their municipality in the case study research project and convinced about its usefulness. Even within the municipalities (Table 4) there were only a few barriers that are perceived unambiguously by all individuals (two authorities with no univocally perceived barrier, three cases with one univocally perceived barrier; only one authority that started the process after an awareness campaign had seven univocally perceived barriers).

**Table 3.** Perceived barriers of all municipalities.

| Barrier | Mean | Range |
|---|---|---|
| Higher demand prerequisite | 3.2245 | 3 |
| Different views | 3.1667 | 3 |
| Additional work | 3.0833 | 3 |
| Uncertain legal position | 2.7778 | 3 |
| Law very complex | 2.7333 | 3 |
| Too expensive | 2.6875 | 3 |
| Follow-up costs not included | 2.6875 | 3 |
| No green alternatives available | 2.6596 | 3 |
| User prejudice | 2.6122 | 3 |
| Difficult to identify | 2.5510 | 3 |
| Possibilities not widely used | 2.5217 | 3 |
| Guidelines do not support | 2.5208 | 3 |
| Administration process hurdle | 2.4898 | 3 |
| Missing information about alternatives | 2.2245 | 3 |
| Not informed about relevance | 2.1458 | 3 |
| Initiatives not encouraged | 2.0612 | 3 |
| Not informed about possibilities | 1.9592 | 3 |
| Legal framework prevents | 1.7955 | 3 |
| Lower functionality | 1.7347 | 3 |
| No aim (of my organization) | 1.5625 | 2 |
| Not informed about aim | 1.4694 | 2 |
| Efforts not useful | 1.1633 | 1 |

**Table 4.** Perceived barriers by the single municipalities.

| | A | | B | | C | | D | | E | | F | |
|---|---|---|---|---|---|---|---|---|---|---|---|---|
| Barrier | Mean | Range | Mean | Range | Mean | Range | Mean | Range | Mean | Range | Mean | Range |
| Efforts not useful | 1.0000 | 0 | 1.6250 | 1 | 1.1667 | 1 | 1.0000 | 0 | 1.2500 | 1 | 1.0000 | 0 |
| No aim (of may organization) | 1.5833 | 2 | 1.1250 | 1 | 1.5000 | 1 | 1.0000 | 0 | 1.8750 | 1 | 1.7500 | 2 |
| Different views | 3.6667 | 1 | 3.8750 | 1 | 2.5000 | 1 | 2.0000 | 2 | 3.2500 | 2 | 2.6667 | 3 |
| Not informed about aim | 1.3333 | 1 | 1.0000 | 0 | 1.8333 | 2 | 1.0000 | 0 | 1.2500 | 1 | 2.0000 | 2 |
| Not informed about possibilities | 1.5000 | 2 | 1.3750 | 2 | 2.0000 | 2 | 1.0000 | 0 | 1.7500 | 2 | 3.1667 | 3 |
| Initiatives not encouraged | 2.0833 | 3 | 1.3750 | 1 | 2.1667 | 1 | 1.3333 | 1 | 1.7500 | 2 | 2.8333 | 3 |
| Guidelines do not support | 2.4167 | 3 | 1.5000 | 2 | 2.8333 | 3 | 3.6667 | 1 | 2.4286 | 2 | 2.9167 | 2 |
| Possibilities not widely used | 2.9091 | 3 | 1.6250 | 2 | 2.0000 | 2 | 1.0000 | 0 | 3.3333 | 2 | 3.0000 | 2 |
| Uncertain legal position | 2.8182 | 3 | 1.8750 | 3 | 3.4000 | 2 | 3.3333 | 2 | 2.8333 | 1 | 2.9167 | 3 |
| Law very complex | 2.6364 | 3 | 2.5000 | 2 | 2.6667 | 2 | 4.0000 | 0 | 3.4000 | 1 | 2.4167 | 3 |
| Legal framework prevents | 2.0000 | 2 | 1.2500 | 1 | 2.0000 | 2 | 2.6667 | 3 | 1.6667 | 2 | 1.7273 | 2 |
| Not informed about relevance | 1.9167 | 2 | 1.3750 | 2 | 1.8333 | 2 | 2.5000 | 1 | 1.7500 | 2 | 3.2500 | 2 |
| Missing information about alternatives | 2.1667 | 2 | 1.3750 | 2 | 1.8333 | 2 | 2.3333 | 2 | 2.2500 | 1 | 3.0000 | 2 |
| Difficult to identify | 2.5000 | 3 | 3.0000 | 2 | 2.6667 | 2 | 1.6667 | 2 | 3.0000 | 2 | 2.1667 | 3 |
| No green alternatives available | 2.2727 | 2 | 2.2500 | 2 | 2.2000 | 1 | 2.6667 | 3 | 3.2500 | 2 | 3.0833 | 3 |
| Too expensive | 2.2500 | 3 | 2.1250 | 1 | 3.0000 | 2 | 2.3333 | 1 | 2.3750 | 3 | 3.6667 | 1 |
| Lower functionality | 1.8333 | 3 | 2.0000 | 2 | 1.8333 | 2 | 1.0000 | 0 | 1.6250 | 2 | 1.6667 | 2 |
| User prejudice | 2.8333 | 3 | 2.8750 | 2 | 2.3333 | 3 | 2.6667 | 3 | 2.6250 | 1 | 2.3333 | 3 |
| Administration process hurdle | 3.2500 | 3 | 2.2500 | 1 | 2.0000 | 2 | 2.3333 | 2 | 2.5000 | 1 | 2.1667 | 3 |
| Additional work | 3.5833 | 2 | 3.0000 | 2 | 2.8000 | 2 | 3.6667 | 1 | 3.2500 | 2 | 2.5000 | 3 |
| Follow-up costs not included | 2.5000 | 2 | 2.8750 | 1 | 2.6000 | 3 | 2.3333 | 3 | 3.2500 | 2 | 2.5000 | 3 |
| Higher demand prerequisite | 2.9167 | 3 | 3.2500 | 1 | 3.8333 | 1 | 2.6667 | 3 | 3.7500 | 1 | 3.0000 | 3 |

On the group level differences emerged, too. For instance, the barrier 'Given possibilities to include environmental criteria are widely used in my municipality (barrier, if not supported)' is perceived as rather high by the finance department, i.e. this group thought that there were more possibilities given than actually used. Moreover, the interviews showed that the perception differed depending on the purchased goods or services, be it furniture, information technology, building equipment, or cleaning services.

In addition, the respondents' rating of their individual influence spreads across the whole scale. These findings indicate a need to differentiate the analysis into multiple levels as 'organisations are multilevel systems' (Klein & Kozlowski, 2000b, p. 3). Limiting the analysis to the organizational level is not sufficient to understand what hinders organizations to implement green practices.

### Stage 2: enfolding literature and deriving hypotheses

Therefore, step 6 focuses on *enfolding the literature* on barriers to greening organizations and multilevel analysis. A variety of barriers are identified by empirical studies (Post & Altman, 1994; Walker et al., 2008). Besides barriers from the external environment, for instance, legal requirements (Brander & Olsthoorn, 2002; Ochoa & Erdmenger, 2003; Ochoa & Guenther, 2005) which forbid the organization to add ecological features in a tender for goods and services, a variety of barriers occurring at the organizational level as well as from the individual level, for instance attitude of personnel, commitment of the management, and communication issues (Post & Altman, 1994), are identified. Consequently, barriers can be considered at the macro as well as at the micro level (Hadjimanolis, 2003). Organizational science has been criticized for thinking either micro or macro and thereby neglecting that both aspects are vital for analysing organizational behaviour (Klein & Kozlowski, 2000a). The micro level perspective, with its psychological origins (Klein & Kozlowski, 2000b), focuses on differing individual characteristics: 'organisations do not behave; people do' (Klein & Kozlowski, 2000b, p. 7). For example, the individual involved in the procurement process might not be willing to support greening organizations because she/he perceives it as additional work (Hanks et al., 2008).

Limiting the barrier analysis to the individual level fails to conduct a comprehensive barrier analysis as a single-level perspective disregards the influences from other levels (Klein & Kozlowski, 2000b). The macro level perspective complements the micro level analysis by concentrating on regularities in social behaviour and other contextual factors (Klein & Kozlowski, 2000b). The organization itself can hamper its greening efforts with conflicting priorities: a low-cost strategy might conflict with buying green products as they might effort a price premium compared to their less ecological alternative (Hanks et al., 2008).

Moreover, limiting the level of analysis to individual, organization, and external environment neglects levels in between, such as different departments and working groups, which represent the group level (Hackman, 2003). Merging the barriers identified in the case study with the literature on multilevel analysis, we group the barriers along the three levels individual, group/organization, and external environment (Figure 2).

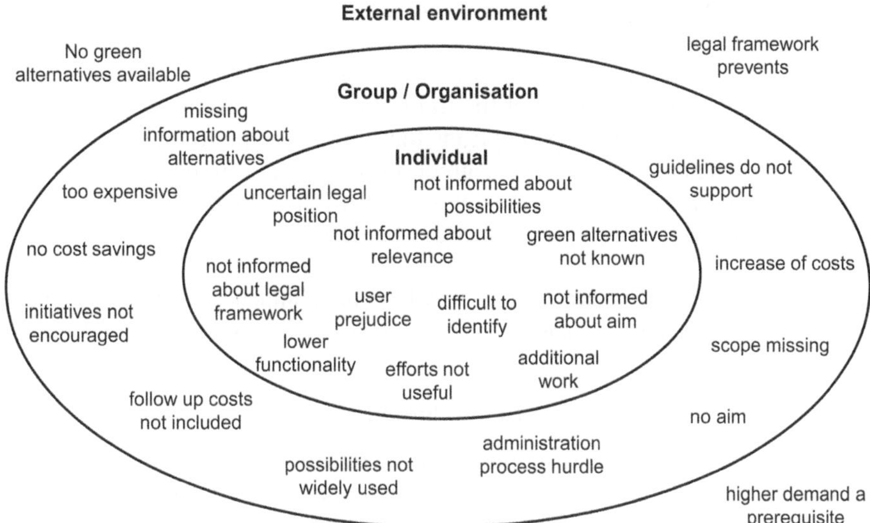


**Figure 2.** Barriers on multiple levels of analysis.

In order to take into consideration the specific characteristics of the group level, we continued our analysis on the group level and focused on the procurement department in order to *shape hypotheses* in step 7. Consequently, we continued our case study analysis on the organizational, group, and individual levels. We added desk research for the external environment.

Following the actors identified in the multiple case study (Figure 1), we focus on the comparison of the strategic and operational levels to differentiate between the perceptions of barriers by managers and by employees (Hadjimanolis, 2003). Individuals are constrained by their role in the organization (Antal, Lenhardt, & Rosenbrock, 2001). According to their involvement in the decision process and their hierarchical power, employees of the strategic level perceive barriers lower than employees on the operational level. Therefore, we deduce the first hypothesis concerning the perception of barriers.

Hypothesis 1: The employees on the strategic level rate barriers lower than the employees at the operational level.

Another form of differentiation on the group level occurs in terms of the different goods and services procured by different departments; therefore, the operational level is further differentiated according to the supplied good or service. Different sub-units happen to develop different sub-cultures that can raise barriers for exchange of expertise between the units and thereby for organizational learning (Antal et al., 2001). The experience with green procurement differs like the features of the procured goods and services: providing catering with fair trade coffee involves different actors and faces different barriers than procuring green office material (Bala et al., 2008). Accounting for those differences, the second hypothesis follows:

Hypothesis 2: Purchasers of different goods and services rate barriers differently.

Besides these differences in position and in procured goods and services, we account for personal differences of the individuals. Each group consists of different individuals with different perceptions that might be due to their attitude, abilities, and experiences. Furthermore, greening organizations might be hampered because one purchaser cannot transfer his knowledge to his colleagues (Antal et al., 2001). So the third hypothesis could be derived:

Hypothesis 3: Purchasers that perceive they have high influence on the procurement process rate barriers lower than purchasers that perceive they have low influence.

### Stage 3: multilevel barriers to green purchasing

These hypotheses are the starting point for the third stage of research: a survey of procurement officials in one of the biggest procurement agencies in Europe. The analysed public authority is in charge of the procurement for federal authorities, foundations, and international organizations. It encompassed one strategic department for central services and seven operational procurement departments, which were specialized according to the type of the requested good or service, for instance, information technology, work clothes, accommodation, and office equipment.

The research focus was on the perceived barriers to green procurement. They emerged from individual perceptions of the actors and can be classified as 'shared properties' (Klein & Kozlowski, 2000b). Therefore, data to measure barriers to green purchasing are assessed by asking the employees for their perception of barriers (Klein & Kozlowski, 2000b). We conducted an online survey among the 220 employees in October/November 2009. Every workplace was equipped with a personal computer so that all employees had the opportunity to participate. The link for the online questionnaire was emailed to the staff via the head of the quality and environmental management department. Fifty-one employees participated in the survey; 9 of those worked in the strategic department and 42 belonged to departments on the operational level which are specialized on procuring different goods and services, such as for instance, information technology equipment, automobiles, office equipment, etc.

Similar to the survey in the first round, the survey consisted of two main sections. The first part focused on the procurement process as a multi-actor process by asking for the function of the participant, the perceived influence on the implementation of green procurement, and the efforts other actors within the company might take to improve green procurement. For the second part, we further developed the questions on barriers by integrating the findings of enfolding the literature. Consequently, we excluded barrier number 22 'Higher demand for environmentally friendly product and services alternatives by users within the municipality is a premise for more environmental procurement' as the individual person of an organization cannot influence the market demand. To deeper analyse if a person could inform themselves about green alternatives because criteria or prices are available or they do not know about green alternatives, we added to the statement 'Information (criteria, prices, and services) concerning green product and service alternatives are available (barrier, if not supported)' the statement 'I am informed about green product and service alternatives (barrier, if not supported)' Moreover, we included the cost-related questions: 'green procurement opens up opportunities for cost savings' and 'green procurement causes cost increases' which already were part of the earlier version of the survey but only as 'yes/no' questions, and 'it is possible to procure green product and service alternatives within a given cost scope (barrier, if not supported)'. According to the interviewed experts we deleted barrier 3 (Table 2) because the 'different views' are included in all statements and changed barrier 10 to 'I am informed about the relevant legal framework for green procurement (barrier, if not supported)'. In the end, we compiled 24 statements to assess the perceived relevance of potential barriers. For the interpretation in this last step 8 of Eisenhardt's framework *reaching closure* we follow the multilevel structure as presented above.

*Organizational level*

Before testing the hypotheses we analysed the perceived barriers for the whole organization regarding their relevance (mean) and whether the barriers were perceived homogenously or heterogeneously (range). Employees of the same investigated organization perceived the prevalence of all barriers (Table 5). The barrier 'no cost savings' (mean: 3.0392) is the most relevant barrier for the surveyed persons. In contrast, the barriers 'efforts not useful' and 'lower functionality' proved to be perceived less as barriers. All other barriers are of medium importance. Moreover, Table 5 reveals that all barriers have a maximum range, which indicates that barriers are perceived very differently in this organization. Those differing perceptions might be caused by different hierarchical levels (see hypothesis 1), by the differences in the nature of the goods and services supplied (see hypothesis 2), or by differences on the individual level (see hypothesis 3).

*Group level: strategic versus operational perspective*

To test hypothesis 1, we distinguished the respondents according to their affiliation to the strategic or operational department (Table 5). We compared the mean rates of the strategic and the operational group for each of the 24 barrier statements using a *t*-test. Table 6 shows only the significant results; for the other barriers no significant difference could be stated. The employees at the strategic level rated all of the listed barriers lower than the employees of the operational level.

According to those results, two main differences between the strategic and the operational level can be stated: (1) the operational level does not significantly agree with the strategic level concerning the following three barriers: green procurement is an aim of the organization, guidelines do not support green procurement, and initiatives are not encouraged. (2) There are different perceptions

**Table 5.** Perceived barriers of the whole organization and distinguished in the strategic and operational level.

| | Whole organization | | Strategic level | | Operational level | |
|---|---|---|---|---|---|---|
| Barrier | Mean | Range | Mean | Range | Mean | Range |
| No cost savings | 3.0392 | 3 | 3.1111 | 1 | 3.0238 | 3 |
| Increase in costs | 2.7647 | 3 | 3.0000 | 2 | 2.7857 | 2 |
| User prejudices | 2.7451 | 3 | 2.7778 | 3 | 2.7619 | 3 |
| Legal framework prevents | 2.7059 | 3 | 2.5556 | 3 | 2.7381 | 3 |
| Follow-up costs not included | 2.6471 | 3 | 2.5556 | 3 | 2.7143 | 3 |
| Uncertain legal position | 2.6471 | 3 | 2.4444 | 3 | 2.7143 | 3 |
| Not informed about legal framework | 2.6471 | 3 | 2.4444 | 1 | 2.6429 | 3 |
| Difficult to identify | 2.5882 | 3 | 2.3333 | 2 | 2.6190 | 3 |
| Not informed about relevance | 2.5490 | 3 | 2.2222 | 1 | 2.6190 | 3 |
| Too expensive | 2.5098 | 3 | 2.2222 | 1 | 2.6190 | 3 |
| Additional work | 2.4902 | 3 | 2.1111 | 2 | 2.5952 | 3 |
| Not informed about aim | 2.4510 | 3 | 2.0000 | 2 | 2.5714 | 3 |
| Not informed about possibilities | 2.4510 | 3 | 2.0000 | 2 | 2.5238 | 3 |
| Administration process hurdle | 2.4118 | 3 | 2.0000 | 3 | 2.5238 | 3 |
| No green alternatives available | 2.4118 | 3 | 1.8889 | 2 | 2.5000 | 3 |
| Possibilities not widely used | 2.3922 | 3 | 1.8889 | 1 | 2.5000 | 3 |
| Missing information about alternatives | 2.3922 | 3 | 1.8889 | 2 | 2.5000 | 3 |
| Initiatives not encouraged | 2.3333 | 3 | 1.8889 | 2 | 2.4048 | 3 |
| Green alternatives not known | 2.2941 | 3 | 1.7778 | 2 | 2.3571 | 3 |
| Guidelines do not support | 2.2745 | 3 | 1.7778 | 2 | 2.3571 | 3 |
| Scope missing | 2.1373 | 3 | 1.6667 | 1 | 2.1905 | 3 |
| No aim (of my organization) | 2.0392 | 3 | 1.6667 | 1 | 2.0952 | 3 |
| Lower functionality | 1.7255 | 3 | 1.4444 | 1 | 1.7857 | 3 |
| Efforts not useful | 1.5490 | 3 | 1.0000 | 0 | 1.6667 | 3 |

**Table 6.** Comparison of means between strategic and operational level.

| Barrier | *t*-value | *p*-value |
|---|---|---|
| No green alternatives available | 2.095 | .041 |
| Efforts not useful | 2.346 | .023 |
| Guidelines do not support | 2.193 | .033 |
| Scope missing | 2.408 | .020 |
| Missing information about alternatives | 2.015 | .049 |
| Not informed about aim | 1.887 | .065 |
| No aim (of my organization) | 3.213 | .002 |
| Initiatives not encouraged | 2.330 | .024 |

between the strategic level and the operational procurement officials on whether alternatives or information are available, which indicates that the strategic level underestimates the supply of green alternatives or that the operational units are missing the tools to identify those alternatives.

**Table 7.** Operational department specialized on information technology compared with all other operational departments.

| Barrier | $t$-value | $p$-value |
|---|---|---|
| Green alternatives not known | −2.345 | .024 |
| Guidelines do not support | −4.490 | .000 |
| Additional work | −1.880 | .067 |
| Scope missing | −1.751 | .088 |
| Not informed about aim | −3.166 | .003 |
| Not informed about possibilities | −3.314 | .002 |
| Not informed about legal framework | −1.912 | .063 |
| Not informed about relevance | −2.173 | .036 |
| No aim (of my organization) | −2.599 | .013 |
| Administration process hurdle | −2.597 | .013 |
| Initiatives not encouraged | −2.497 | .017 |

*Group level: characteristics of procured goods or services*

The aggregated results of the operational departments (Table 5) still show a high heterogeneity. This goes along with our argumentation for our hypothesis 2 that purchasers of different goods and services rate barriers differently. This could be proved for example for the department which procures information technology. This department shows significantly different means for 11 barriers when comparing it with the other operational departments (Table 7).

The department for aeronautics and the department for services and technical equipment show also significant means for several barriers.

The comparison of the other groups revealed that in the department services of print and digital media just one barrier, namely 'additional work', has a significantly lower mean and in the department clothing and furnishings only the

**Table 8.** Pearson correlation ($r$) between 'own influence' and barriers.

| Barrier | $r$ | $p$-value |
|---|---|---|
| Green alternatives not known | −.442 | .001 |
| No green alternatives available | −.358 | .010 |
| Efforts not useful | −.315 | .024 |
| Guidelines do not support | −.473 | .000 |
| Additional work | −.371 | .007 |
| Scope missing | −.307 | .028 |
| Legal framework prevents | −.401 | .004 |
| Missing information about alternatives | −.433 | .002 |
| Not informed about possibilities | −.497 | .000 |
| Not informed about legal framework | −.283 | .044 |
| Not informed about relevance | −.322 | .021 |
| No aim (of my organization) | −.450 | .001 |
| Administration process hurdle | −.387 | .005 |
| Initiatives not encouraged | −.293 | .037 |
| Increase in costs | .270 | .055 |

barrier 'not informed about the relevance' has a significantly lower mean. In the department communication and electronic technology and the department tools and equipment, no barrier shows any significant different mean.

*Individual level: perceived barriers versus perceived influence*

To test hypothesis 3 'purchasers that perceive themselves to have high influence on the procurement process rate barriers lower than purchasers which perceive themselves to have low influence' we examined the relationship between variable 'own influence' and all barriers. The variable 'own influence' has a significant correlation with almost all barriers. Table 8 presents that the correlation is negative in all but one case, which means that the higher a person rates their 'own influence', the lower the person perceives the barriers. The positive correlation appears at the barrier 'increase in costs'. These results show that the individual perceived barriers are linked to the perceived own influence of the interviewee. Therefore, further barrier research should account for the individual as a level of analysis.

## Conclusion

The analysis of barriers to green purchasing gives valuable insights into the greening of organizations. Based on multiple case studies, a tool to identify and analyse barriers to green procurement in the public sector was developed and tested. The findings highlight the relevance of multilevel research. Distinguishing individual, group, organization, and external environment as levels of analysis contributes to our understanding of the 'why not' perspective on fostering green management.

These results provide helpful insights for researchers and practitioners. Investigations to identify barriers should include the perspective of managers as well as employees to avoid biased results and to allow a comprehensive understanding. Managers should be aware that their perception might differ from the barriers perceived by the employees who are involved in greening the organization by modifying their day-to-day business according to green standards.

In addition, the findings on green procurement distinguished according to the procured goods and services indicate an influence for the greening activity. Barriers can differ depending on the subject of greening.

The case studies are limited to the investigation of perceived barriers, which may not be the real barriers. For instance, the legislation is perceived as hampering green procurement, but at the supranational level the legal frameworks for green procurement are given. Thus, the procurer might not be aware of the current legal framework. Moreover, it is difficult to differentiate between barriers on the organizational or group level and those on the individual level; for example, employees of the organizational level are of the opinion that green procurement is not an aim of the organization, which can arise due to bad communication within the organization. In summary, we conclude that the 'why not' perspective can be the starting point for the 'how to' perspective to develop strategies that overcome the barriers towards greening organizations.

## References


Antal, A. B., Lenhardt, U., & Rosenbrock, R. (2001). Barriers to organizational learning. In M. Dierkes, A. B. Antal, J. Child, & I. Nonaka (Eds.), *Organizational learning and knowledge* (pp. 865–885). Oxford: Oxford University Press.

Bala, A., Munoz, P., Rieradevall, J., & Ysern, P. (2008). Experiences with greening suppliers. The Universitat Autonoma de Barcelona. *Journal of Cleaner Production, 16*(15), 1610–1619.

Boiral, O. (2009). Greening the corporation through organizational citizenship behaviors. *Journal of Business Ethics, 87*(2), 221–236.

Brammer, S., & Walker, H. (2007). *Sustainable procurement practice in the public sector: An international comparative study* (Working Paper Series 2007.16). Bath: University of Bath, School of Management.

Brander, L., & Olsthoorn, X. (2002). Three scenarios for green public procurement. *IVM Paper W, 2*, 1–36.

Brief, A. P., & Motowidlo, S. J. (1986). Prosocial organizational behaviors. *Academy of Management Review, 11*(4), 710–725.

Cunningham, J. B., & Kempling, J. S. (2009). Implementing change in public sector organizations. *Management Decision, 47*(2), 330–344.

Daily, B. F., Bishop, J. W., & Govindarajulu, N. (2009). A conceptual model for organizational citizenship behavior directed toward the environment. *Business & Society, 48*(2), 243–256.

Defranceschi, P., & Hidson, M. (2007). The potential of GPP for the spreading of new/recently developed environmental technologies – Case studies. In Oeko-Institut e. V.; Local Governments for Sustainability (ICLEI) (Eds.), *Costs and benefits of green public procurement in Europe* (pp. 1–122). Freiburg. Retrieved from http://kozbeszerzes.hu/static/uploaded/document/eu_recommendations.pdf.

Eisenhardt, K. M. (1989). Building theories from case study research. *Academy of Management Review, 14*(4), 532–550.

Geng, Y., & Doberstein, B. (2008). Greening government procurement in developing countries: Building capacity in China. *Journal of Environmental Management, 88*(4), 932–938.

Guenther, E., Greschner Farkavcová, V., & Scheibe, L. (2010). The hurdle analysis as an instrument for improving sustainable stewardship. *Management Research Review, 33*(4), 340–356.

Guenther, E., & Scheibe, L. (2006). The hurdle analysis. A self-evaluation tool for municipalities to identify, analyse and overcome hurdles to green procurement. *Corporate Social Responsibility & Environmental Management, 13*(2), 61–77.

Guenther, E., & Scheibe, L. (2005). The hurdle analysis as an instrument for improving environmental value chain management. *Progress in Industrial Ecology – An International Journal, 2*(1), 107–131.

Hackman, J. R. (2003). Learning more by crossing levels: Evidence from airplanes, hospitals, and orchestras. *Journal of Organizational Behavior, 24*(8), 905–922.

Hadjimanolis, A. (2003). The barriers approach to innovation. In L.V. Shavinina (Ed.), *The international handbook on innovation* (pp. 559–573). Oxford: Pergamon.

Hanks, J., Davies, H., & Perera, O. (2008). *Sustainable public procurement in South Africa.* Winnipeg: International Institute for Sustainable Development.

Hart, S. L. (1995). A natural-resource-based view of the firm. *Academy of Management Review, 20*(4), 986–1014.

Henriques, I., & Sadorsky, P. (1999). The relationship between environmental commitment and managerial perceptions of stakeholder importance. *Academy of Management Journal, 42*(1), 87–99.

Klein, K. J., & Kozlowski, S. W. J. (2000a). From micro to meso: Critical steps in conceptualizing and conducting multilevel research. *Organizational Research Methods, 3*(3), 211–236.

Klein, K. J., & Kozlowski, S. W. J. (2000b). A multilevel approach to theory and research in organization. Contextual, temporal, and emergent processes. In K. J. Klein & S. W. J. Kozlowski (Eds.), *Multilevel theory, research, and methods in organizations: Foundations, extensions, and new directions* (pp. 3–90). San Francisco, CA: Jossey-Bass.

Løland Dolva, C. (2007). *Green public procurement (GPP): How widespread is green public procurement in Norway, and what factors are seen as drivers and barriers to a greener procurement practice?* Stockholm. Retrieved from http://www.stockholmresilience.org/download/18.aeea46911a31274279800078675/

McWilliams, A., & Siegel, D. (2000). Corporate social responsibility and financial performance: Correlation or misspecification? *Strategic Management Journal, 21*(5), 603–609.

Murray, J. G. (2000). Effects of a green purchasing strategy: The case of Belfast city council. *Supply Chain Management: An International Journal, 5*(1), 37–44.

Ochoa, A., & Erdmenger, C. (2003). *Study contract to survey the state of play of green public procurement in the European Union.* Freiburg: International Council for Local Environmental Initiatives.

Ochoa, A., & Guenther, D. (2005). Umweltfreundliche Beschaffung in Europa – Ergebnisse einer Befragung unter öffentlichen Beschaffern [Green Procurement in Europe – Results of a survey among public procurers]. In R. Barth, C. Erdmenger, & E. Guenther (Eds.), *Umweltfreundliche Beschaffung. Innovationspotentiale, Hemmnisse, Strategien [Green public procurement. Innovation potentials, barriers, strategies]* (pp. 23–31). Heidelberg: Physica-Verlag.

OECD (ed.). (2007). *Improving the environmental performance of public procurement: Report on Implementation of the Council Recommendation. OECD Papers, 7*(9), 1–36. Retrieved from http://dx.doi.org/10.1787/oecd_papers-v7-art26-en

Parliament House of Commons Environmental Audit Committee (EAC) (ed.). (2005). *Sustainable procurement. Sixth report of session 2004–05.* London. Retrieved from http://www.publications.parliament.uk/pa/cm200405/cmselect/cmenvaud/266/266.pdf.

Post, J. E., & Altman, B. W. (1994). Managing the environmental change process: Barriers and opportunities. *Journal of Organizational Change Management, 7*(4), 64–81.

Ren, T. (2009). Barriers and drivers for process innovation in the petrochemical industry: A case study. *Journal of Engineering and Technology Management, 26*(4), 285–304.

Steurer, R., Berger, G., Konrad, A., & Martinuzzi, A. (2007). *Sustainable public procurement in EU member states: Overview of government initiatives and selected cases.* Vienna: Final Report to the EU High-Level Group on CSR.

Thun, J., & Müller, A. (2010). An empirical analysis of green supply chain management in the German automotive industry. *Business Strategy and the Environment, 19*(2), 119–132.

Walker, H., & Brammer, S. (2007). *Sustainability procurement in the United Kingdom public sector* (Working Paper Series 2007.15). Bath: University of Bath, School of Management.

Walker, H., Di Sisto, L., & McBain, D. (2008). Drivers and barriers to environmental supply chain management practices: Lessons from the public and private sectors. *Journal of Purchasing & Supply Management, 14*(1), 69–85.

Wirtz, B., Lutje, S., & Schierz, P. G. (2010). An empirical analysis of the acceptance of e-procurement in the German public sector. *International Journal of Public Administration, 33*(1), 26–42.

Yin, R. K. (2003). *Case study research. Design and methods.* 3rd ed. Thousand Oaks, CA/London/Delhi: Sage.

# The Good, the Bad, and the Successful – How Corporate Social Responsibility Leads to Competitive Advantage and Organizational Transformation

ANDRÉ MARTINUZZI & BARBARA KRUMAY

*Institute for Managing Sustainability, Vienna University of Economics and Business, Austria*

ABSTRACT *This paper presents a referential stage model for corporate social responsibility (CSR) implementation by linking CSR to four business operations: project management, quality management, strategic management and organizational learning. Companies try to cope with societal demands by integrating them into these business operations: (1) integrating societal demands into project management by initiating a project in an area that is perceived as 'good'; (2) avoid 'bad things' by applying quality management for CSR implementation; (3) strategic CSR perceives societal demands as opportunities to create shared value and (4) transformational CSR helps to overcome constraints like low materiality and developing the capabilities of a company. While the first two stages aim at 'doing good' or 'avoiding bad', strategic and transformational CSR are key for 'being successful'. Based on extended literature review and well-documented studies, our referential framework offers insights into underlying patterns, potentials and limitations of linking CSR to business operations. Companies can assess the stage they have reached, strive for higher materiality, boost their competitiveness, and evolve in terms of CSR maturity. Hence, the referential framework adds a new and application-oriented perspective to the discussion of the business case for CSR and demonstrates how stages lead to competitive advantage and organizational transformation.*

## 1. Introduction

In our conceptual paper, we describe three common approaches – project-oriented corporate social responsibility (CSR), quality-oriented CSR, and strategic CSR – based on a comprehensive literature review and selected cases. Opportunities for and threats to an individual company as well as to society are assessed. Furthermore, we identify a fourth approach based on organizational learning, which is, in our impression, the logical next step for companies willing to act in a responsible way.

The Good: CSR is often seen as 'doing good'. Businesses make donations to civil society and environmental organizations, sponsor projects in developing countries, build solar power units, spend money on counselling for employees, etc. These projects are commonly perceived as 'good', and are thus easy to communicate to the general public. However, such projects remain peripheral and are in danger of being cancelled in times of crisis.

The Bad: Many companies face severe problems when they are revealed to use child labour in their supply chain, to be accountable for environmental disasters, or to ignore human rights. In such cases, consumers' loyalty is quickly jeopardized, and even the license to operate can be endangered. CSR can therefore be seen as preventing 'doing bad'. To help companies in implementing this approach, several standards, management systems, and checklists were developed. However, it is difficult to say to what extent a single company can be held accountable in a globalized economy. In addition, checklists and standards are often difficult to communicate to customers.

... and The Successful: CSR can also be seen as a strategic success factor and an opportunity to create shared value. The challenge is to take social and environmental issues into account and to 'rethink your business' around four strategic questions: what, where, how, and for whom are we producing? This creates new business models, boosts incentive innovation, and builds up a robust reputation.

On the basis of this literature study, we identified a fourth innovative approach to link CSR with change management and organizational learning: 'transformational CSR'. The paper structure is as follows: first we describe the relationship between CSR and competitive advantage, as well as our research aim and methodological approach. Second, we explore how linking of CSR with business operation leads to a logical and sound categorization of stages of CSR, which can be achieved often in companies, as demonstrated by different cases. And finally, we present conclusions and an outlook on the next steps.

## 2. CSR and Competitive Advantage

In recent years, the concept of CSR has become established increasingly all over the world: more than 260,000 companies worldwide have implemented a certified environmental management system following ISO14001 (ISO, 2004b); about 4,500 organizations make use of the European Eco-Management and Auditing Scheme (European Commission, 2005); about 8,000 businesses and non-business stakeholders from 135 countries participate in the UN-driven

Global Compact initiative; 42 of the most developed countries, which account for 85% of the total foreign direct investment flow, have established National Contact Points for promotion and diffusion of the Organisation for Economic Co-operation and Development (OECD) 'Guidelines for Multinational Enterprises' (OECD, 2011); the Social Accountability standard SA8000 has been implemented in 62 countries covering about 3,000 facilities and about 1.5 million workers (SAI, 2008); and about 1,500 companies have published CSR reports based on the guidelines of the Global Reporting Initiative (GRI, 2011).

Explaining and assessing CSR are hampered by the fact that a broad variety of terms evolved in research, which all deal with rather similar corporate activities. But even when the same term is used, there is still the potential for seeing the concept from different angles, applying competing conceptual frameworks, and discussing them in different research communities (e.g. corporate sustainability, business ethics, stakeholder management, corporate citizenship, corporate governance, and shared value). Researchers applied different methodological approaches to explain and define CSR: from summarizing existing definitions (Carroll, 1999; Carter & Jennings, 2004; Joyner & Payne, 2002; Moir, 2001), over analysing research papers (Dahlsrud, 2008; Montiel, 2008; Taneja, Taneja, & Gupta, 2011), and to conducting interviews (Johnston & Beatson, 2005; O'Dwyer, 2002). Some researchers developed a CSR definition based on theoretical reasoning (Göbbels, 2002; Matten & Crane, 2005a; Van Marrewijk, 2003). Nevertheless, some key ideas are applied most commonly:

- CSR is the obligation of business to act according to the overarching goals of the society. Hence, it is connected with sustainable development as CSR's guiding vision.
- CSR depends on the political, institutional, and cultural context and environment, as it is dependent on the relationship between business and society.
- CSR is beyond compliance: A precondition to responsible corporate behaviour is to be compliant to laws or regulations.
- CSR is voluntary (since it is beyond compliance), but it is still perceived as a moral, ethical, or philanthropic obligation of business, although some labour unions and Non Governmental Organizations (NGOs) are constantly questioning the voluntariness of CSR.
- Making profit out of CSR: It is questioned if making profits out of CSR can still be perceived as CSR. Is it immoral to make money out of being moral? Seen from a different angle, the following question arises: Can CSR measures that do not have any – even indirect – influence on profit be regarded as CSR – for example, is philanthropy a form of CSR? This is an on-going debate.

These key ideas can be applied at the policy level as well. For a long period, CSR was experienced as an active corporate engagement beyond legal compliance and the voluntary contribution of business to the overall guiding societal model of sustainable development (European Commission, 2001, 2002, 2008). Since the recent CSR Communication of the European Union published in October 2011 (European Commission, 2011), which states that CSR is the responsibility of every company for its impacts on the environment and society, the idea of CSR has been changing. CSR has become a concern for all businesses, independent of their sizes, sectors, or locations.

One big issue in the CSR debate, already discussed for a long time, is the question of whether or not CSR leads to improved competitiveness (Carroll & Shabana, 2010). A number of studies concerning the 'business case of CSR' tried to validate the relationship between CSR and competitive advantage. As a result, a majority of these studies support the idea that a positive relationship between CSR and competitive advantage exists (Becchetti, Ciciretti, Hasan, & Kobeissi, 2012; Clarkson, Li, Richardson, & Vasvari, 2008; Ghoul, Guedhami, Kwok, & Mishra, 2011; Sharfman & Fernando, 2008; Vilanova, Lozano, & Arenas, 2009), but some studies presented contrary results (Cordeiro & Sarkis, 1997; Hassel, Nilsson, & Nyquist, 2005). In addition, some found the relationship to be neutral (Nelling & Webb, 2009; Wagner, 2005). These equivocal results lead to a number of meta-studies based on the existing literature (Griffin & Mahon, 1997; Guenther, Hoppe, & Endrikat, 2011; Margolis & Walsh, 2003; Orlitzky, Schmidt, & Rynes, 2003). Some of them (Orlitzky et al., 2003) supported the idea that under certain circumstances (e.g. increasing reputation), CSR is mutually reinforcing: improved CSR (respectively, corporate social performance) may actually lead to more competitiveness (respectively, corporate financial performance) and improved competitiveness enables the implementations of CSR measures. However, the intermediate factors and their role to make this reinforcement happen are just sketched on a very vague basis, hence this relationship will further be investigated.

## 3. Research Aim and Methodological Approach

Our research aim is to shed light onto the rather vaguely described linkage of CSR and competitiveness. Compared with other approaches (Carroll, 1999; Carter & Jennings, 2004; Dahlsrud, 2008; Göbbels, 2002; Johnston & Beatson, 2005; Joyner & Payne, 2002; Matten & Crane, 2005b; Moir, 2001; Montiel, 2008; O'Dwyer, 2002; Taneja et al., 2011; Van Marrewijk, 2003), our typology presents a referential framework to analyse different stages of CSR implementation, focusing on the materiality of CSR and helping to assess the potential of CSR to create competitive advantage and new business opportunities. It links CSR to four of the most frequently implemented business operations:

- Project-oriented CSR: Projects are seen as a temporary organization and a social system different from permanent organization. They are designed for the performance of a relatively unique, short- to medium-term strategic business process of medium or large scope. Since CSR activities are often integrated into projects and handled by project management, we identified this as the first and easiest way of integrating CSR into a standard business operation.
- Quality-oriented CSR: Quality management has a long tradition in research and practice and is often connected to standards such as ISO or total quality management (TQM). Within these standards, CSR is gaining importance. Hence, we identified quality management as the second important business operation in which CSR can be integrated.

- Strategic CSR: Strategic management influences organizations since the long-term approach and the positioning of the organization in competition are inherent in strategy. Since CSR is approached strategically, the success of the whole organization may increase. Therefore, we see strategic management as our third business operation.
- Transformational CSR: Organizational learning and change does not only have the potential to change the organization and transform it from a static, reactive company to a dynamic, self-learning organization. It also allows the parallel transformation of an organization, its stakeholders, and the whole society. Therefore, we will sketch transformational CSR as the fourth and most powerful approach to implement CSR.

Our conceptual paper is based on a literature review and the analysis of selected case studies, which are well documented in scholarly literature and the media. We focus on proactive business operations and hence excluded defensive or finance-related operations (e.g. risk management, which is also often connected to CSR). The four business operations in our stage model were identified based on this analysis. In the following sections, we explain how these business operations integrate or embed CSR, why they are predominant in the CSR literature, and why they can be found in companies very often.

## 4. Linking CSR with Business Operations

Already in the late 1970s, Carroll (1979) presented stages or phases of social responsiveness, ranging from no response to pro-active response. Moreover, he framed different stages in his ground-breaking CSR pyramid, from economic (be profitable), to legal (obey the law), to ethical (be ethical), and up to philanthropic (be a good corporate citizen) responsibilities of a company (Carroll, 1991) and hence presented a first stage model of CSR. Another early stage model is Frederick's CSR1/CSR2/CSR3/CSR4 concept (Frederick, 1978, 1986, 1998). He describes the development from the rather philosophical CSR1, which is the obligation of a company to 'work for social betterment', to a managerial concept, which is more action-oriented – CSR2, and includes the ability of a company to react on social pressure (Frederick, 1978). Later he concluded from his research that the concepts need an ethical basis and hence presented Social Corporate Rectitude (CSR3), which enables a constant surveillance of the impact of companies' actions on society. This was further developed into CSR4 to overcome the 'CSR1–2–3 trap' having the company in the centre of CSR (Frederick, 1998).

Other authors presented different phases or stages, e.g. Dunphy (2002), who elaborated six stages of sustainability. Crowther (2008) identified seven stages and described them in terms of dominant features. Halme and Laurila (2009) presented a model with higher complexity, showing three stages, from reactive or defensive, driven by the demand of external influences, to a strategic and transformative orientation, as well as three CSR types with three dimensions. Baumgartner and Ebner (2010) presented four stages of corporate sustainability strategies or sustainability profiles: beginning, elementary, satisfying, and sophisticated/

outstanding. Another way of seeing CSR is provided by Schneider (2012), who defines several system boundaries of CSR development stages, and determines four stages from social engagement without systematic and planned behaviour (CSR 0.0) to a proactive political designer (CSR 3.0). In order to systematize this variety of CSR stage models, two systematic reviews have recently been carried out: Spitzeck and Hansen (2011) elaborated different ways of measuring or describing CSR based on historical, performance-based, structural, cognitive, and moral-cognitive measures. Maon, Lindgreen, and Swaen (2010) developed a consolidative model based on nine other stage models and presented seven stages describing the development from 'CSR-unsupportive to CSR-supportive cultures through its development of integrated CSR programmes and policies'.

Different researchers critically discussed stage models for CSR or sustainability. They criticize, for example, that the complexity of the current situation of a company can never be represented by such stages (Kolk & Mauser, 2001), especially since national, international, and global regimes are very different. Others note that guidelines for overcoming hurdles to reach a higher stage are rarely integrated into the models or lack integration with existing business processes (Asif, Searcy, Zutshi, & Fisscher, 2013). Nonetheless, stage models support researchers and practitioners to identify the situation that a company is in, to make companies comparable to each other by identifying and measuring the characteristics of the stages, to offer insights into best practice cases in the stage, and to offer the possibility of developing measures to either act as best as possible in the situation or identify necessary steps to reach a higher stage (Asif et al., 2013; Baumgartner & Ebner, 2010; Maon et al., 2010; Panwar, Rinne, Hansen, & Juslin, 2006).

Although CSR stage models are numerous and many authors see a connection between the stages and business operations (Halme & Laurila, 2009), hardly any of them are directly linked to business operations, but instead are based on theoretical concepts and considerations. Therefore, they are not integrated into core business processes (Asif et al., 2013). In addition, most of them present defensive versus proactive attitudes of businesses towards CSR and sustainable development as a key element and, therefore, do not offer more complex insights into the practical problems of CSR implementation. Our paper is meant to help understand different stages of integrating CSR into existing business operations, their strengths and weaknesses, opportunities and threats. In our approach, 'higher stages' build upon and integrate the characteristics of 'lower' stages some overlaps between stages are logical. Next, we present the different stages and explain the specific characteristics of the stages.[1]

### *4.1 Project-Oriented CSR ('Doing Good')*

Projects and project management are adopted and implemented by many organizations. Definitions of projects range from a project being an idea or draft (Engwall, 1998), a complex task (IPMA, 2006; PMI, 2008), a complex system to be optimized (Cleland & King, 1983), a social entity (Thamhain, 2004), a legal unit (Barnes, 1983), a business objective (Pinto & Slevin, 1987), or a temporary organization (Turner & Müller, 2003). Gareis defines a project as a temporary organization and a social system different from permanent organization, designed for the performance of a relatively unique, short- to medium-term strategic business process of medium or large scope (Gareis, 2005). Hence, project management is a process different from the content of the project, and is used for 'planning, organizing, and managing resources to bring about the successful completion of a specific project' (Vyas, 2008).

Many companies approach CSR by initiating a social or environmental project, and thus aim at 'doing good'. The projects' content varies from targeting customers (e.g. cause-related marketing), external stakeholders (e.g. sponsorships, awards, donations), or internal stakeholders (e.g. voluntary social or health services, corporate volunteering). The following examples give just a brief insight into the great variety of project-oriented CSR:

- Simacek Facility Management Group GmbH[2] in Austria initiated a project in cooperation with a non-profit organization to support their employees in learning German. Since most of their employees are migrants and very often have no command of the language of the country they live in, this is a way to foster integration and social stability of employees. The courses are voluntary and correlated with working hours.
- Coca Cola in Austria together with the NPO Competence Center of the Vienna University of Economics and Business and the newspaper *Der Standard* initiated a project called 'Ideen gegen Armut' (ideas fighting poverty).[3] This project invites people to introduce their ideas on how to fight poverty, and supports needy people to help themselves by bringing up new business ideas. The company awards about 100,000 euros per year to implement the best idea.
- RHI,[4] a producer of refractory materials, installed a new waste heat concept where the air used for cooling of the tunnel kiln fosters as an energy source for machines and water treatment, which results in reducing the consumption of fossil energy of 2,317 tons of carbon dioxide.

All of these projects are undoubtedly 'good', which makes them easily communicable to the public. However, they are not necessarily in the focus of the companies' activities and are often the first to be cancelled in times of economic crisis. As project-oriented CSR often means to give back a certain share of the profit to society, several questions arise concerning this allocation decision: (1) is it the obligation of companies to spend profit for society, or should businesses purely concentrate in business, (2) what is the right amount (e.g. is it sufficient to allocate a few thousand euros for 'being good' or is there a minimum to be 'really good'?), (3) who should benefit from 'doing good' (e.g. fighting poverty or protecting rare species?), (4) how will other stakeholders not benefiting from the project perceive the initiative? For example, when the Deutsche Bank fired 10% of their employees (Deutsche Bank, 2003), one might have asked why the company still spent money in fighting AIDS in Asia (Deutsche Bank, 2006).

We consider project-oriented CSR as the first stage due to the nature of projects. Projects have a limited duration, they start and end with a fixed goal and budget (Gareis, Huemann, & Martinuzzi, 2011). This means that at a certain point they are finished and do not influence the company as a whole. In addition, communicating sponsorship and donations is easy. An organizational change, especially in culture and processes of the company, does not necessarily take place in this stage. Consequently, project-oriented CSR is just a first step towards sustainable management, and hence further steps are required to transform responsibility into success for companies. Due to the nature of projects, which have limited timeframe and resources often linked to middle management, societal and economic impacts are low, but also risks are not very high. Furthermore, the materiality is low because after the project ends, it does not need further managerial actions. To summarize this stage, we could define it as the stage where companies strive for 'doing good' and integrate this aim into projects and project management.

### *4.2 Quality-Oriented CSR ('Avoid Doing Bad!')*

Quality management has been a well-known concept for decades. At the very beginning, quality thinking aimed at the quality of products and services, but further developed to quality of production and service processes, quality of the whole production system to overall quality of the organization (van der Wiele, Kok, Mckenna, & Brown, 2001).

> Quality management is defined as an integrated approach to achieving and sustaining high quality output, focusing on the maintenance and continuous improvement of processes and defect prevention at all levels and in all functions of the organization, in order to meet or exceed customer expectations. (Flynn, Schroeder, & Sakakibara, 1994)

To apply quality management, standardized management systems, quality guidelines and standards, audits, or assessments are used. One approach to assess quality is TQM, which has been developed to foster 'an all-embracing philosophy of conceptual Business Excellence' (Robson & Mitchell, 2007). It is an integrated approach that aims to continuously improve the quality of products or services of a company (Hackman & Wageman, 1995; Porter & Parker, 1993; Powell, 1995; Sureshchandar, Rajendran, & Anantharaman, 2001). Many quality management tools already include CSR measurement (Robson & Mitchell, 2007), such as the ISO9000/9001 (ISO, 2005) for quality, ISO14000/14001 (ISO, 2004a) for Eco-Management, or ISO26000/260001 (ISO, 2010)[5] or Eco-Management and Audit Scheme (European Commission, 2005) – either explicitly or implicitly.

Companies applied environmental management systems (e.g. following the ISO14001 series) as a next step after implementing quality management systems (e.g. following the ISO9001 series). The lately developed ISO26000 can be perceived as a third step in this sequence, although the focus shifted from management systems standards to guidance standards (Castka & Balzarova, 2007). The majority of these companies applied a quality-oriented approach to protect their image, brand, and license to operate, as famous cases showed how quickly reputation is lost and regained by applying quality measures:

- In the textile industry, companies such as Nike or Deichmann suffered from image-damaging reports about poor working conditions in their supply chains and developed codes of conduct to rebuild trust in their responsibility (DeTienne & Lewis, 2005; Loew, 2005).
- Unfair practices and poor working conditions led to a loss in credibility in the retail sector, as the case of Lidl, a cut-price supermarket chain, showed. As reported by the newspaper Stern,[6] the company spied on its staff and collected intimate information concerning their staff's relationships, habits, and how often the employees used their mobile phones during their breaks (Walsh & Bartikowski, in press).
- In the oil industry, the Shell versus Greenpeace case on the dismantling of the Brent Spar oil platform demonstrated how quickly reputation was lost (Zyglidopoulos, 2002). The recent BP Deepwater Horizon case proved that minor errors (i.e. a failing blowout preventer with costs of about 400,000 dollars) can cause major damages (i.e. more than 20 billion dollars) (Lewis, 2011).

These cases depict how quickly reputation may get lost and even the license to operate might be in danger. Therefore, many companies implemented quality management systems and standards to reduce these threats in their own operations, preferred suppliers who implemented these standards, or developed codes of conduct. However, it is not an easy task to avoid 'bad things', particularly due to the fact that the idea of 'avoiding bad things' is diverse, highly relative, and has an emotional component. When there is evidence that a company uses child labour to produce their goods, that dramatic ecological devastation is an effect of production, or that they ignore human rights, it seems to be an easy decision. But how far does the responsibility of a single company go (i.e. how many tiers of suppliers)? And how can companies find a balance between their own ethical standards and the cultural conditions in other countries (e.g. the right of workers to organize labour unions is rather limited in several countries)?

We consider quality-oriented CSR as a second stage, which is even more complex and fosters some changes in the structures and processes of an organization. In implementing quality management systems or following quality management guidelines, a company has to look at business processes and restructure them. The materiality of this approach is, therefore, higher. Furthermore, the different quality management schemes require validation and re-auditing, which helps to develop a more professional approach to CSR than just initiating a single project. Advantages of implementing quality-oriented CSR are given by the standardized and well-defined nature of quality management instruments. By applying such instruments, organizations are able to identify and describe their status as well as report their achievements in implementing CSR. Drawbacks of this stage are manifold, for example, the problem to communicate the value of management systems to the public. Moreover, quality management systems with their checklists are often seen as annoying obligations, and the resulting stimulus for innovation is rather low. Quality-oriented CSR ensures a systematic approach, but needs extension by other steps towards corporate sustainability, as managing responsibilities is more complex than managing quality (Waddock & Bodwell, 2004).

### *4.3 Strategic CSR ('Rethink Your Business!')*

Modern companies are using business or corporate strategy to position and distinguish themselves from competitors. Although the strategy already emerged as an important discipline in the 1970s (Carter, Clegg, & Kornberger, 2010), it is diversely discussed in the literature and a single definition is still missing. Porter (1996), for example, sees strategy as the way in which companies can perform activities distinctive from those of their rivals, and how they may position themselves uniquely, either based on customers' needs, customers' accessibility, or the companies' products or services. Mintzberg states that strategy does not have one definition, but five: it is a plan, a pattern, a position, a perspective, and a ploy (Mintzberg, Ahlstrand, & Lampel, 2005). Strategic management is often connected to other concepts, such as the relationship between power and strategy (Carter et al., 2010). Basically – agreed upon by researchers and practitioners – strategy is long-term, sets directions, and defines a company's position (Bowman & Helfat, 2001; Mintzberg et al., 2005; Porter, 1996). In addition, strategic management is not a one-way road, but includes formulation, implementation, and control in cascading steps (Mintzberg et al., 2005), and influences projects as well as quality management processes in a company. A business strategy describes how a company competes and positions itself (Bowman & Helfat, 2001), whereas corporate strategy 'defines the businesses in which a company will compete, preferably in a way that focuses resources to convert distinctive competence into competitive advantage' (Andrews, 1987).

The aim of strategic CSR is to include environment and society in strategic decisions and to open up an innovation potential. Thus, CSR is integrated into all four central business decisions: what, where, how, and for whom the company is producing. This holistic penetration of CSR enables new business models and leads the company's innovation capacity to the very target of social problems and their solutions. Strategic CSR as a term is used in different ways, e.g. as a socially responsible profit-maximizing strategy (Baron, 2001; Bhattacharyya, 2010; Porter & Kramer, 2006). Hence, the relationship between the success of the company and the societal impacts of strategic CSR is perceived as mutually reinforcing (Porter & Kramer, 2006). Strategic CSR includes mission and vision statements (Lantos, 2001), requires decisions (Porter & Kramer, 2006), and targets stakeholders, especially consumers, employees, and marketers (Lantos, 2001). Husted and Salazar (2006) compared different approaches (strategy, altruism, and coerced egoism) and state that a strategic CSR approach is superior to the others based on calculating costs, benefits, and social output. Examples of strategic CSR are versatile and impressive:

- Muhammed Yunus (Nobel Peace Prize Laureate) started a micro-credit initiative with the Grameen Bank in Bangladesh in the 1970s (Yunus, Moingeon, & Lehmann-Ortega, 2010; Yunus & Weber, 2007). This initiative reached a volume of 60 billion US-dollars. The loans are issued to small-scale traders with an amount of credits of 1,000 US-dollars each (Yunus & Weber, 2007). These micro-credits enable the deployment of independent businesses in developing countries and foster the reduction of poverty.

- Betapharm, a pharmaceutical manufacturer producing generic drugs, enriched its corporate activities by founding a network of facilities for seriously and chronically ill children and their families offering a broad variety of prevention, care, and post-rehabilitation support. Instead of investing in the development of new drugs or investigating the prescription behaviour of medical practitioners, Betapharm supported ill children and gained broad knowledge about their living arrangements (Heuskel, 2008).
- Some software-producing companies such as Specialisterne[7] and Aspiritech[8] (Johnson, 2011) deploy people with Asperger syndrome, a form of autism, to test the software. They are able to find errors five times faster than IT-experts. They are not seen as handicapped people who should be integrated just on the edge of society. On the contrary, the company established highly specialized, high-quality, and highly paid jobs which match the strengths and needs of people with autism (Cammuso, 2011; Mottron, 2011).

As these examples show, 'rethink your business' is the motto of strategic CSR. Strategic CSR unlocks shared value by investing in social aspects of context and strengthening a company's competitiveness (Porter & Kramer, 2011) and by helping to achieve a generic firm strategy, new products, and markets based on social and economic inclusion (Bhattacharyya, 2010). It can be assessed as a source of tremendous social progress (Porter & Kramer, 2006). The high potential impact of strategic decisions is simultaneously the biggest constraint of strategic CSR: the successful history of a company, existing structures and processes, and narrow patterns of thought form the most important barriers to innovation and change. These problems are caused by the enormous influence that the changes can have on the company and the stakeholders involved (Yuan, Bao, & Verbeke, 2011). As a consequence, measuring the effectiveness and impacts of strategic CSR is difficult, as at the moment societal and environmental concerns are fully integrated into the core decisions of a company. CSR as such can no longer be easily identified, but can be seen as a new, integrated form of CSR, creating shared value for the company and the society.

We consider strategic CSR as the third stage towards linking CSR and competitiveness, as it helps to develop an overall strategy, improves stakeholder relations, and creates shared value. The on-going changes involved in implementing strategic CSR are profound, since this means that CSR is integrated into business or corporate strategy. The changes are not short- or mid-term, but long-term, and influence the company as a whole. Processes must be adopted, employees have to be informed about the strategy, and a certain commitment to CSR is required. Therefore, the materiality is high. There are certain risks when integrating CSR into strategy, such as losing the position achieved in the market or upsetting business partners. The abilities that are necessary in order to overcome these constraints are in the focus of the next CSR approach, which very rarely can be found in companies.

### *4.4 Transformational CSR ('Stay Flexible!')*

'CSR involves learning over time and the ability to understand the specific context and confluence of stakeholder expectations' (Maon, Lindgreen, & Swaen, 2009), hence organizational learning and transformation as well as stakeholder integration are strongly linked with CSR issues. Organizational learning addresses strategy, structure, and culture of a company and the system as a whole (D'Amato & Roome, 2009). Companies face changing requirements in a constantly changing world, and hence have to react in a flexible way (Roome & Louche, 2011). By adapting to the situation and integrating (social, economic, and environmental) requirements into the learning process, they are in a continuous, result-open (and hence iterative) process, which is the basis for sustainable competitiveness and strengthening the resilience of companies. This organizational learning and transformation already includes communication mechanisms, hence stakeholder dialogues, stakeholder engagement, and stakeholder management – additional leading topics in the CSR discussion (von Weltzien Hoivik, 2011) – are vital. Involving stakeholders enables an organization to contribute to the wealth and sustainable development of the organization itself and the (social and natural) environment in which it is embedded (Donaldson & Preston, 1995; Freeman, 1984; Frooman, 1999; Mainardes, Alves, & Raposo, 2011; Mitchell, Agle, & Wood, 1997). Since stakeholder involvement is an important issue, research has addressed it accordingly. Stakeholder management seeks to support the relationship and communication between the organization and internal or external stakeholders (Carroll & Buchholtz, 2011). Johansen and Nielsen (2011) developed a literature-based framework to explore and support understanding of stakeholder dialogue by targeting issues of responsibility and legitimacy. Nijhof, De Bruijn, and Honders (2008) emphasized the role of NGOs for the success of businesses in CSR and identified three strategies in this area, which are unbalanced or even controversial in terms of goals and concerns of companies and NGOs. Wals and Schwarzin (2012) state in a conceptual paper that dialogic interaction is necessary to enable transition towards organizational sustainability as well as to achieve sustainability competence. This dialogue may be institutionalized and includes alliances between non-profit and for-profit actors, which in turn enable learning in organizations (Arya & Salk, 2006).

Since organizational learning and transformation include participatory mechanisms which enable not only employees, but also external stakeholders to influence an organization's development, both concepts are closely related and can be integrated into 'transformational CSR' (for details see Martinuzzi & Zwirner, 2010). Examples of transformational CSR are rare and often highlight just one aspect of the complex interplay of change, learning, and transformation:

- A longitudinal study in two hospitals in London showed that changes in working, relationships, and leadership are necessary to develop the abilities of learning. However, the changes have to be embedded into the organizational culture to be sustainable (Mitleton-Kelly, 2011).

- The Arla Foods-consumer dialogue was implemented by offering a portal to strengthen relationships with Danish consumers. The portal presented frequently asked questions coupled with feedback, based on the idea that stakeholders engage with organizations. Via feedback and dialogue, stakeholders are involved and mutual commitment can be achieved (Johansen & Nielsen, 2011).
- Sabaf, a world-leading manufacturer of components for domestic gas cooking appliances, embedded social, environmental, and governance issues. To develop a new approach to CSR, the company runs through a transformation process that includes learning and change processes in the company (Roome & Louche, 2011).

We consider transformational CSR as the fourth stage, which is able to overcome some constraints of the preceding stages such as narrow-mindedness, inflexibility, or sticking to standardized ways. An organization which is able to learn and transform based on experiences and collected knowledge that integrates CSR in this transformation is flexible, and may adapt quickly to new challenges and gains competitive advantage (Vilanova et al., 2009). Moreover, this organization contributes to societal change and acts as a key driver for sustainable business practices, which also can be seen as a competitive advantage. As this could lead to a transformation of economic and political framework conditions (e.g. through establishing new environmental or social standards or through contributing to a change of values in society such as 'sufficiency' instead of 'greed'), the assessment of the competitive advantage of transformational CSR is not easy. On the one hand, changing the 'rules of the game' might lead to an outstanding position; on the other hand, the predictability of these changes is very low. Transformational CSR, therefore, does not focus on gaining a specific competitive advantage by implementing CSR, but on fostering the abilities, which form the basis of these advantages: the ability of an organization to develop its capabilities for reacting in a flexible way on social, ecological, and economical requirements and to continue with progress.

## 5. Conclusion

In this paper, we sketched a stage model based on three most often implemented business operations linked to CSR, i.e. project management, quality management, and strategic management, as well as an additional approach – organizational learning and change. While the first three are well described in scholarly papers, the fourth is rather innovative as it puts the linkages of CSR and competitiveness in a dynamic and even systemic perspective. When entering a new stage, the characteristics of the previous stages of course are still existing and integrated into the higher stages (e.g. CSR projects of 'doing good', quality management measures of 'avoid doing bad'), hence the characteristics are not mutually exclusive, but the company's approach to CSR reaches another level. The following figure shows our stage model encompassing the four approaches described above (Figure 1).

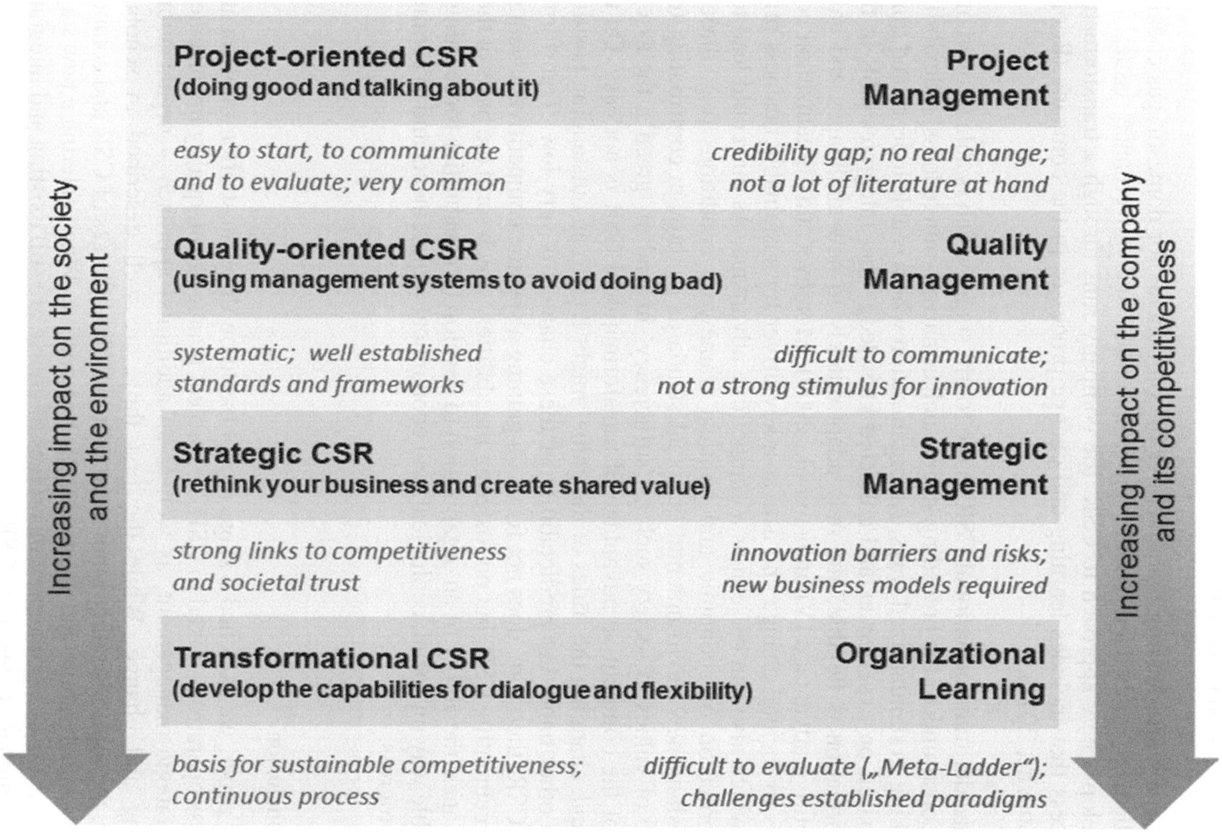

Increasing impact on the society and the environment

**Project-oriented CSR**
**(doing good and talking about it)**

**Project Management**

*easy to start, to communicate and to evaluate; very common*

*credibility gap; no real change; not a lot of literature at hand*

**Quality-oriented CSR**
**(using management systems to avoid doing bad)**

**Quality Management**

*systematic; well established standards and frameworks*

*difficult to communicate; not a strong stimulus for innovation*

**Strategic CSR**
**(rethink your business and create shared value)**

**Strategic Management**

*strong links to competitiveness and societal trust*

*innovation barriers and risks; new business models required*

**Transformational CSR**
**(develop the capabilities for dialogue and flexibility)**

**Organizational Learning**

*basis for sustainable competitiveness; continuous process*

*difficult to evaluate („Meta-Ladder"); challenges established paradigms*

Increasing impact on the company and its competitiveness

**Figure 1.** CSR stage model.

A first evaluation of the applicability of our stage model was done in two research projects as a guiding framework for interviews with CSR sectoral experts and in the course of a Delphi-like survey, and received interesting results:

- In the construction sector, three actors play a prominent role in shaping the environmental and societal impacts of construction on the one hand, and deciding on its costs structure on the other: the property developer, the general contractor, and the future user. Only if at least one of these key actors requires them, CSR measures are implemented. If none of them perceives CSR measures as essential, societal responsibility is seen in contradiction to the high pressure for low costs, which are the most decisive factor for competitiveness in this sector (Martinuzzi, Gisch-Boie, & Wiman, 2010). This leads to the situation that the same company might apply CSR on a very high level at one construction site (when it is required by one of the three key actors), while in another construction project CSR issues are ignored to reduce costs. We consider this sector to be in the stage of project-oriented CSR.
- In the chemical industry, quality-oriented CSR is the most common approach: ISO14001 and Responsible Care are the best-established CSR tools. Experts see several positive links of CSR and competitiveness and believe that CSR will gain importance in the future. However, the relevance of CSR as a source of competitive advantage is rather limited, as other issues like innovation, product quality, and human resources are of much higher importance for competitiveness. Therefore, the life-cycle approach, safeguarding the license to operate, and socially responsible human resource management are perceived as pathways for strategic CSR in the chemical sector.

As the examples show, the stage model presented here can be used as a framework to assess the recent situation of a company and of a whole sector, respectively. Therefore, it might be applied in the course of upcoming empirical projects as well as in the course of consulting projects.

As stated in the paper, the stage model offers a way to assess how companies develop in the course of time. The characteristics of the stages based on the underlying business operations may be used to answer some questions: concerning competitiveness, we argue that the competitiveness of the company increases by entering higher CSR stages. The changes in the organizations walking along this path are very different, reaching from being slightly unchanged (project-oriented CSR) to a stage where recurring changes and learning are the basis for success (transformational CSR). Since responsibility of companies is growing or transforming into shared value, the positive impact on society will increase by entering higher stages.

Since this model is in a conceptual stage, we consider the following research issues as most promising to pursue: (1) the further development of the four stages to a fully fledged maturity model for CSR, including the development of indicators to assess the stages more clearly, (2) the application in surveys to assess the maturity of certain sectors, (3) a series of case studies to deepen the understanding of the contingencies and constraints of the four stages, and (4) some accompanying research projects on cases where individual companies managed to shift from one stage to another.

### Acknowledgements

The authors thank Wilhelm Zwirner for his support in developing the transformational CSR approach; Robert Kudlak and Michal Sedlacko for valuable input; and Bernhard Nussgruber and Megan Ahearn for proofreading.

### Funding

The authors thank the Austrian National Bank for funding project number 13175, which made this paper possible.

### Notes

1. The development of indicators based on the characteristics is part of ongoing research.
2. http://www.simacek.com/en
3. http://www.ideen-gegen-armut.at
4. http://www.rhi.at/internet_en
5. Other ISO systems (ISO10001 for customer satisfaction and complaints systems, ISO31000 for risk management, AA1000 for sustainability assurance, ISO26000 for corporate responsibility and SA8000 for social accountability) related to CSR and sustainability are not that popular (Asif et al., 2013).
6. http://www.stern.de/wirtschaft/news/unternehmen/studie-spitzelskandal-ramponiert-lidl-image-654199.html
7. http://specialisterne.com
8. http://www.aspiritech.com

### References

Andrews, K. R. (1987). *The concept of corporate strategy*. New York: Richard D. Irwin.

Arya, B., & Salk, J. E. (2006). Cross-sector alliance learning and effectiveness of voluntary codes of corporate social responsibility. *Business Ethics Quarterly*, *16*(1), 211–234.

Asif, M., Searcy, C., Zutshi, A., & Fisscher, O. A. M. (2013). An integrated management systems approach to corporate social responsibility. *Journal of Cleaner Production*, *56*, 7–17.

Barnes, M. (1983). How to allocate risks in construction contracts. *International Journal of Project Management*, *1*(1), 24–28.

Baron, D. P. (2001). Private politics, corporate social responsibility, and integrated strategy. *Journal of Economics & Management Strategy*, *10*(1), 7–45.

Baumgartner, R. J., & Ebner, D. (2010). Corporate sustainability strategies: Sustainability profiles and maturity levels. *Sustainable Development*, *18*(2), 76–89.

Becchetti, L., Ciciretti, R., Hasan, I., & Kobeissi, N. (2012). Corporate social responsibility and shareholder's value. *Journal of Business Research*, *65*(11), 1628–1635.

Bhattacharyya, S. S. (2010). Exploring the concept of strategic corporate social responsibility for an integrated perspective. *European Business Review*, *22*(1), 82–101.

Bowman, E. H., & Helfat, C. E. (2001). Does corporate strategy matter? *Strategic Management Journal*, *22*(1), 1–23.

Cammuso, K. (2011). Inclusion of students with autism spectrum disorders. *The Brown University Child and Adolescent Behavior Letter*, *27*(11), 1–8.

Carroll, A. B. (1979). A three-dimensional conceptual model of corporate performance. *Academy of Management Review*, *4*(4), 497–505.

Carroll, A. B. (1991). The pyramid of corporate social responsibility: Toward the moral management of organizational stakeholders. *Business Horizons*, *34*(4), 39–48.

Carroll, A. B. (1999). Corporate social responsibility. *Business & Society, 38*(3), 268–295.

Carroll, A. B., & Buchholtz, A. K. (2011). *Business and society: Ethics and stakeholder management*. Dallas, TX: South-Western Cengage Learning.

Carroll, A. B., & Shabana, K. M. (2010). The business case for corporate social responsibility: A review of concepts, research and practice. *International Journal of Management Reviews, 12*(1), 85–105.

Carter, C., Clegg, S., & Kornberger, M. (2010). Re-framing strategy: Power, politics and accounting. *Accounting, Auditing & Accountability Journal, 23*(5), 573–594.

Carter, C., & Jennings, M. (2004). The role of purchasing in the socially responsible management of the supply chain: A structural equation analysis. *Journal of Business Logistics, 25*(1), 145–186.

Castka, P., & Balzarova, M. (2007). A critical look on quality through CSR lenses. *The International Journal of Quality & Reliability Management, 24*(7), 738–752.

Clarkson, P. M., Li, Y., Richardson, G. D., & Vasvari, F. P. (2008). Revisiting the relation between environmental performance and environmental disclosure: An empirical analysis. *Accounting, Organizations and Society, 33*(4), 303–327.

Cleland, D. I., & King, W. R. (1983). *Systems analysis and project management*. New York: McGraw-Hill (McGraw-Hill series in management).

Cordeiro, J. J., & Sarkis, J. (1997). Environmental proactivism and firm performance: Evidence from security analyst earnings forecasts. *Business Strategy and the Environment, 6*(2), 104–114.

Crowther, D. (2008). The maturing of corporate social responsibility: A developmental process. In D. Crowther & N. Capaldi (Eds.), *The Ashgate research companion to corporate social responsibility* (pp. 19–30). Ashgate: New Orleans.

Dahlsrud, A. (2008). How corporate social responsibility is defined: An analysis of 37 definitions. *Corporate Social Responsibility and Environmental Management, 15*(1), 1–13.

D'amato, A., & Roome, N. (2009). Toward an integrated model of leadership for corporate responsibility and sustainable development: A process model of corporate responsibility beyond management innovation. *Corporate Governance, 9*(4), 421–434.

Detienne, K. B., & Lewis, L. W. (2005). The pragmatic and ethical barriers to corporate social responsibility disclosure: The Nike case. *Journal of Business Ethics, 60*(4), 359–376.

Deutsche Bank. (2003). *Deutsche Bank annual report 2003*. Retrieved October 22, 2011, from http://www.db.com/ir/en/download/db_ar03_annual_report_2003.pdf

Deutsche Bank. (2006). *Creating Deutsche Bank Asia Foundation 2003–2005*. Retrieved October 22, 2011, from www.db.com/csr/de/docs/eng_csr-report-asien_2003_2005.pdf

Donaldson, T., & Preston, L. E. (1995). The stakeholder theory of the corporation: Concepts, evidence, and implications. *Academy of Management Review, 20*(1), 65–91.

Dunphy, D. (2002). *Organizational change for corporate sustainability*. London: Routledge.

Engwall, M. (1998). The project concept(s): On the unit of analysis in the study of project management. In R. A. Lundin & C. Midler (Eds.), *Projects as arenas for renewal and learning processes* (pp. 25–35). Boston, MA: Kluwer Academic Publishers.

European Commission. (2001). *Green paper – Promoting a European framework for corporate social responsibility. COM (2001)*. Brussels: Commission of the European Communities.

European Commission. (2002). *Corporate social responsibility: A business contribution to sustainable development. COM (2002)*. Brussels: Commission of the European Communities.

European Commission. (2005). *EMAS (European Eco-Management and Audit Scheme)*. Brussels: Author.

European Commission. (2008). *Accompanying document to the communication from the Commission on the European Competitiveness Report. (2008). Commission staff working document. COM (2008)*. Brussels: Commission of the European Communities.

European Commission. (2011). *A renewed EU strategy 2011–14 for corporate social responsibility*. Brussels: Author.

Flynn, B. B., Schroeder, R. G., & Sakakibara, S. (1994). A framework for quality management research and an associated measurement instrument. *Journal of Operations Management, 11*(4), 339–366.

Frederick, W. (1978). From CSR1 to CSR2: The maturing of business and society thought, working paper 279, Graduate School of Business, University of Pittsburgh (re-published in 1994). *Business & Society, 33*(2), 150–164.

Frederick, W. (1986). Toward CSR3: Why ethical analysis is indispensable and avoidable in ethical affairs. *California Management Review, 28*(2), 12–25.

Frederick, W. (1998). Moving to CSR4. *Business and Society Review, 37*(1), 40–59.

Freeman, R. E. (1984). *Strategic management: A stakeholder approach.* Boston, MA: Pitman.

Frooman, J. (1999). Stakeholder influence strategies. *Academy of Management Review, 24*(2), 191–205.

Gareis, R. (2005). *Happy Projects!* Vienna: Manz.

Gareis, R., Huemann, M., & Martinuzzi, A. (2011). *What can project management learn from considering sustainability principles?* Project perspectives 2011 – The Annual Publication of International Project Management Association, XXXIII, pp. 60–65.

Ghoul, S. E., Guedhami, O., Kwok, C. C. Y., & Mishra, D. R. (2011). Does corporate social responsibility affect the cost of capital? *Journal of Banking & Finance, 35*(9), 2388–2406.

Göbbels, M. (2002). Reframing corporate social responsibility: The contemporary conception of a fuzzy notion. *Journal of Business Ethics, 44*, 95–105.

GRI. (2011). *Sustainability reporting statistics.* Retrieved October 22, 2011, from http://www.globalreporting.org/NR/rdonlyres/EDEB16A0-34EC-422F-8C17-57BA6E635812/0/GRIReportingStats.pdf

Griffin, J. J., & Mahon, J. F. (1997). The corporate social performance and corporate financial performance debate: Twenty-five years of incomparable research. *Business & Society, 36*(1), 5–13.

Guenther, E., Hoppe, H., & Endrikat, J. (2011). Corporate financial performance and corporate environmental performance: A perfect match? *Zeitschrift für Umweltpolitik und Umweltrecht, 34*(3), 279–296.

Hackman, J. R., & Wageman, R. (1995). Total quality management: Empirical, conceptual, and practical issues. *Administrative Science Quarterly, 40*, 309–342.

Halme, M., & Laurila, J. (2009). Philanthropy, integration or innovation? Exploring the financial and societal outcomes of different types of corporate responsibility. *Journal of Business Ethics, 84*(3), 325–339.

Hassel, L., Nilsson, H., & Nyquist, S. (2005). The value relevance of environmental performance. *European Accounting Review, 14*, 41–62.

Heuskel, D. (2008). Ausblick: Von der sozialen zur strategischen Perspektive - ein hoffnungsvoller Ausblick zur Zukunft der CSR. In A. Habisch, M. Neureiter, & R. Schmidpeter (Eds.), *Handbuch corporate citizenship* (pp. 519–521). Berlin: Springer.

Husted, B. W., & Salazar, J. (2006). Taking Friedman seriously: Maximizing profits and social performance. *Journal of Management Studies, 43*(1), 75–91.

IPMA. (2006). *International competency baseline* (3rd ed.). Zurich: International Organization for Standardization.

ISO. (2004a). *ISO14000.* Retrieved from http://www.iso.org/iso/iso_14000_essentials

ISO. (2004b). *ISO14001:2004 – Environmental management systems – Requirements with guidance for use.* Geneva: Author.

ISO. (2005). *ISO9000.* Retrieved from http://www.iso.org/iso/iso_9000_essentials

ISO. (2010). *ISO26000.* Retrieved from http://www.iso.org/iso/social_responsibility

Johansen, T. S., & Nielsen, A. E. (2011). Strategic stakeholder dialogues: A discursive perspective on relationship building. *Corporate Communications: An International Journal, 16*(3), 204–217.

Johnson, C. R. (2011). *Autism traits prove valuable for software testing.* Retrieved October 10, 2011, from http://www.smartertechnology.com/index2.php?option=content&do_pdf=1&id=1115

Johnston, K., & Beatson, A. (2005). Managerial conceptualisations of corporate social responsibility: An exploratory study. *Australian and New Zealand Marketing Academy ANZMAC*, Fremantel.

Joyner, B., & Payne, D. (2002). Evolution and implementation: A study of values, business ethics and corporate social responsibility. *Journal of Business Ethics, 41*(4), 297–311.

Kolk, A., & Mauser, A. (2001). The evolution of environmental management: From stage models to performance evaluation. *Business Strategy and the Environment, 11*(1), 14–31.

Lantos, G. P. (2001). The boundaries of strategic corporate social responsibility. *Journal of Consumer Marketing, 18*(7), 595–632.

Lewis, S. (2011). Lessons on corporate 'sustainability' disclosure from Deepwater Horizon. *NEW SOLUTIONS: A Journal of Environmental and Occupational Health Policy, 21*(2), 197–214.

Loew, T. (2005). *CSR in der Supply Chain: Herausforderungen und Ansatzpunkte für Unternehmen.* Berlin: Institute for Sustainability. Retrieved October 17, 2011, from http://www.4sustainability.de/fileadmin/redakteur/bilder/Publikationen/Loew_2006_CSR_in_der_Supply-Chain.pdf

Mainardes, E. W., Alves, H., & Raposo, M. (2011). Stakeholder theory: Issues to resolve. *Management Decision, 49*(2), 226–252.

Maon, F., Lindgreen, A., & Swaen, V. (2009). Designing and implementing corporate social responsibility: An integrative framework grounded in theory and practice. *Journal of Business Ethics, 87*, 71–89.

Maon, F., Lindgreen, A., & Swaen, V. (2010). Organizational stages and cultural phases: A critical review and a consolidative model of corporate social responsibility development. *International Journal of Management Reviews*, *12*(1), 20–38.

Margolis, J. D., & Walsh, J. P. (2003). Misery loves companies: Rethinking social initiatives by business. *Administrative Science Quarterly*, *48*(2), 265–305.

Martinuzzi, A., Gisch-Boie, S., & Wiman, A. (2010). Does corporate responsibility pay off? Exploring the links between CSR and competitiveness in Europe's industrial sectors. *Final report of the project no ENTR/2008/031, 'Responsible Competitiveness' on behalf of the European Commission, Directorate-General for Enterprise and Industry*, Vienna.

Martinuzzi, A., & Zwirner, W. (2010). Transformational CSR – How innovation, organizational learning and stakeholder dialogues support corporate sustainability. In H. Prammer (Ed.), *Corporate sustainability* (pp. 155–174). Wiesbaden, Germany: Gabler.

Matten, D., & Crane, A. (2005a). Corporate citizenship: Toward an extended theoretical conceptualization. *The Academy of Management Review*, *30*(1), 166–179.

Matten, D., & Crane, A. (2005b). Corporate citizenship: Toward an extended theoretical conceptualization. *Academy of Management Review*, *30*(1), 156–176.

Mintzberg, H., Ahlstrand, B., & Lampel, J. (2005). *Strategy safari: A guided tour through the wilds of strategic management*. New York: The Free Press.

Mitchell, R. K., Agle, B. R., & Wood, D. J. (1997). Toward a theory of stakeholder identification and salience: Defining the principle of who and what really counts. *Academy of Management Review*, *22*(4), 853–886.

Mitleton-Kelly, E. (2011). A complexity theory approach to sustainability: A longitudinal study in two London NHS hospitals. *The Learning Organization*, *18*(1), 45–53.

Moir, L. (2001). What do we mean by corporate social responsibility? *Corporate Governance*, *1*, 16–23.

Montiel, I. (2008). Corporate social responsibility and corporate sustainability: Separate pasts, common futures. *Organizational Environment*, *21*(3), 245–269.

Mottron, L. (2011). Changing perceptions: The power of autism. *Nature*, *479*(7371), 33–35.

Nelling, E., & Webb, E. (2009). Corporate social responsibility and financial performance: The 'Virtuous Circle' revisited. *Review of Quantitative Finance and Accounting*, *32*(2), 197–209.

Nijhof, A., De Bruijn, T., & Honders, H. (2008). Partnerships for corporate social responsibility: A review of concepts and strategic options. *Management Decision*, *46*(1), 152–167.

O'dwyer, B. (2002). Conceptions of corporate social responsibility: The nature of managerial capture. *Accounting, Auditing and Accountability Journal*, *16*(4), 523–557.

OECD. (2011). *OECD guidelines for multinational enterprises*. Paris: Author.

Orlitzky, M., Schmidt, F. L., & Rynes, S. L. (2003). Corporate social and financial performance: A meta-analysis. *Organization Studies*, *24*(3), 403–441.

Panwar, R., Rinne, T., Hansen, E., & Juslin, H. (2006). Corporate responsibility: Balancing economic, environmental, and social issues in the forest products industry. *Forest Products Journal*, *56*(2), 4–12.

Pinto, J. K., & Slevin, D. P. (1987). Critical factors in successful project implementation. *IEEE Transactions of Engineering Management*, *EM34*(1), 22–27.

PMI. (2008). *A guide to the project management body of knowledge (PMBoK Guide)* (3rd ed.). Newtown Square, PA: Author.

Porter, L. J., & Parker, A. J. (1993). Total quality management – The critical success factors. *Total Quality Management*, *4*(1), 13–22.

Porter, M. E. (1996). What is strategy? *Harvard Business Review*, *74*(6), 61–78.

Porter, M. E., & Kramer, M. R. (2006). The link between competitive advantage and corporate social responsibility. *Harvard Business Review*, *84*(12), 78–92.

Porter, M. E., & Kramer, M. R. (2011). Creating shared value. *Harvard Business Review*, *89*(2), 62–77.

Powell, T. C. (1995). Total quality management as competitive advantage: A review and empirical study. *Strategic Management Journal*, *16*(1), 15–37.

Robson, A., & Mitchell, E. (2007). CSR performance: Driven by TQM implementation, size, sector? *International Journal of Quality & Reliability Management*, *24*(7), 722–737.

Roome, N., & Louche, C. (2011). Sabaf: Moving to a learning environment. *Journal of Management Development*, *30*(10), 1049–1066.

SAI. (2008). *SA8000*. New York: SAI Social Accountability International.

Schneider, A. (2012). Reifegradmodell CSR - eine Begriffsklärung und -abgrenzung. In A. Schneider & R. Schmidpeter (Eds.), *Corporate social responsibility* (pp. 17–38). Berlin: Springer.

Sharfman, M. P., & Fernando, C. S. (2008). Environmental risk management and the cost of capital. *Strategic Management Journal, 29*(6), 569–592.

Spitzeck, H., & Hansen, E. (2011). *Corporate responsibility evolution models: Concepts, evidence and implications.* Lisbon: EGOS Colloquium.

Sureshchandar, G. S., Rajendran, C., & Anantharaman, R. N. (2001). A conceptual model for total quality management in service organizations. *Total Quality Management, 12*(3), 343–363.

Taneja, S., Taneja, P., & Gupta, R. (2011). Researches in corporate social responsibility: A review of shifting focus, paradigms, and methodologies. *Journal of Business Ethics, 101*, 343–364.

Thamhain, H. J. (2004). Linkages of project environment to performance: Lessons for team leadership. *International Journal of Project Management, 22*(7), 533–544.

Turner, J. R., & Müller, R. (2003). On the nature of the project as a temporary organization. *International Journal of Project Management, 21*(1), 1–8.

Van Der Wiele, T., Kok, P., Mckenna, R., & Brown, A. (2001). A corporate social responsibility audit within a quality management framework. *Journal of Business Ethics, 31*(4), 285–297.

Van Marrewijk, M. (2003). Concepts and definitions of CSR and corporate sustainability: Between agency and communion. *Journal of Business Ethics, 44*(2), 95–105.

Vilanova, M., Lozano, J. M., & Arenas, D. (2009). Exploring the nature of the relationship between CSR and competitiveness. *Journal of Business Ethics, 87*, 57–69.

Von Weltzien Hoivik, H. (2011). Embedding CSR as a learning and knowledge creating process: The case for SMEs in Norway. *Journal of Management Development, 30*(10), 1067–1084.

Vyas, N. (2008). Environmental aspects of project management. *VIKALPA, 33*(2), 65–70.

Waddock, S., & Bodwell, C. (2004). Managing responsibility: What can be learned from the quality movement? *California Management Review, 47*(1), 25–37.

Wagner, M. (2005). How to reconcile environmental and economic performance to improve corporate sustainability: Corporate environmental strategies in the European paper industry. *Journal of Environmental Management, 79*, 105–118.

Wals, A. E. J., & Schwarzin, L. (2012). Fostering organizational sustainability through dialogic interaction. *The Learning Organization, 19*(1), 11–27.

Walsh, G., & Bartikowski, B. (in press). Exploring corporate ability and social responsibility associations as antecedents of customer satisfaction cross-culturally. *Journal of Business Research*, 1–7.

Yuan, W., Bao, Y., & Verbeke, A. (2011). Integrating CSR initiatives in business: An organizing framework. *Journal of Business Ethics, 101*(1), 75–92.

Yunus, M., Moingeon, B., & Lehmann-Ortega, L. (2010). Building social business models: Lessons from the Grameen experience. *Long Range Planning, 43*(2–3), 308–325.

Yunus, M., & Weber, K. (2007). *Creating a world without poverty: Social business and the future of capitalism.* New York: Public Affairs.

Zyglidopoulos, S. C. (2002). The social and environmental responsibilities of multinationals: Evidence from the Brent Spar case. *Journal of Business Ethics, 36*(1), 141–151.

# The Political Ecology of Palm Oil Production

RENATO J. ORSATO*, STEWART R. CLEGG**,† & HORACIO FALCÃO‡

**São Paulo School of Management (EAESP) and Centre for Sustainability Studies (GVces), Getulio Vargas Foundation (FGV), São Paulo, Brazil, **Centre for Management and Organisation Studies (CMOS) and Management Discipline Group, University of Technology, Sydney, Australia, †Nova School of Business and Economics, Lisboa, Portugal, ‡INSEAD Asia Campus, Singapore, Singapore*

ABSTRACT *The paper analyses the social and environmental issues involved in disputes relating to the sustainability of the palm oil industry. These disputes have been aired in and around the Roundtable on Sustainable Palm Oil. We start by developing a review of types of voluntary environmental initiative or green clubs, as they have also been called, in this context. The study is based on extensive fieldwork in the setting of the disputes (the island of Borneo) and analysis of the different levels in the global value chain of the palm oil industry, including local organizations, the industry structure overall, as well as the local governments of Malaysia and Indonesia. The use of the political ecology framework for the analysis of the palm oil industry contributes not only to the development of a more institutional-power perspective, but also provides solid grounds for the understanding of green clubs – an increasingly important type of organization.*

## 1. Introduction

Palm oil has become a controversial commodity. While it is a renewable (bio) fuel and is used as raw material for thousands of products, in the past decades it has also been identified as a major cause of deforestation and loss of biodiversity in Southeast Asia. The island of Borneo is a particular example. Until the 1970s, it was almost entirely covered by tropical forests but in the past decades logging, agriculture and mining have resulted in massive deforestation in part to provide land for palm oil plantations. Deforestation has significantly reduced the only habitat of the orang-utan and other species, such as the pygmy elephant, clouded leopard, Sumatran rhino and other lesser known animals, as well as thousands of species of plants, which may disappear altogether within the next 20 years. The remaining forests are under extreme threat.

Until 1997, the environmental degradation of Borneo had not become an issue in either public opinion or politics. In that year, however, fires that had been set to clear land for palm oil plantations engulfed the whole region of Malaysia and Indonesia with dense smoke, causing respiratory problems and creating an international public outcry. The smoke drifted far, polluting distant cities such as Singapore. The link between deforestation and palm oil was established in the media. Eco-activist and non-governmental organizations (NGOs) that had been campaigning against deforestation and logging in the region exploited the momentum by intensifying campaigns against large organizations involved in the value chain of palm oil. The industry rapidly responded to the attacks and public outcry by organizing a multi-stakeholder coalition led by the largest players in the sector and launched the Roundtable on Sustainable Palm Oil (RSPO).

The RSPO is exemplary of thousands of similar initiatives that have emerged in the past three decades, which scholars (for instance: Prakash & Potoski, 2006) term as *green clubs*. While environmentalists tend to view such coalitions with scepticism, green clubs have been praised for promoting proactive sustainability management. While such opposing views divide opinion, studies of the formation of such clubs are relatively scarce (for a review of the literature in the field, see Orsato, 2009; Vogel, 2006). In their review, Prakash and Potoski (2012) stated that it is still unclear if the extent of the public benefits claimed for green clubs are largely a function of industry self-interest in positive representations rather than something that makes a substantial difference. King and Lenox (2000) and King, Lenox, and Terlaack (2005), in particular, question whether mass participation of firms in green clubs leads to higher aggregate effects of pollution prevention.

The paper analyses the main actors and the disputes between those seeking to preserve the forests of Borneo and those expanding palm oil production. It does so using a theoretical framework initially proposed by Orsato and Clegg (1999). We apply the *political ecology framework* to analysis of the case of eco-activism in the palm oil value chain. The research represents a direct response to the need for neo-institutional theory to incorporate a 'balanced attention to both the influence of the institutional environment and the role of organizational self-interest and active agency within that environment' (Hoffman, 2001, p. 134). By uncovering the political disputes that occur in the formation stage of an important green club, we provide grounds for a proper evaluation. The use of the political ecology framework enables us to explain the *institutional wars* (White, 1992) fought by stakeholders in the field (DiMaggio & Powell, 1983) defining what constitutes 'sustainable palm oil'.

The research is based on a longitudinal case study of agricultural and industrial activities around the palm oil value chain. The data were collected over the period 2008–2010 and in fieldwork during 2009, involving participant observant of agricultural practices and semi-structured interviews with key players in the organizational field, as well as extensive documentary analysis.[1] Before delving deep into the specific case of the green club of the palm oil industry (RSPO), the following section briefly reviews the evolution of green clubs and analyses their reputational value. Sections 3, 4 and 5 provide the context in which the disputes and trades-offs emerged with the expansion of palm oil plantations in Malaysia and Indonesia. In Section 6, we apply the political ecology framework to delve deep into the power disputes involved in the development of the RSPO and Section 7 presents the conclusions of our study.

## 2. Green Clubs

Since the early days of industrialism, laws and other forms of regulation, such as codes of practice, have attempted to make firms accountable for the pollution and other negative externalities they produce. Although they have been effective to a certain extent, the complexity of regulatory rulebooks, enforcement costs and rigidity have limited the effectiveness of such methods of pollution prevention and control (Borck & Coglianese, 2009; Fiorino, 2006; Prakash & Potoski, 2012). As a result, in trying to avoid compliance costs altogether, many corporations have looked for *pollution havens* – countries with more relaxed regulatory frameworks or weak enforcement capabilities (Antweiller, Copeland, & Taylor, 2001).

Large-scale disasters in the 1980s, most notably the explosion of the Bhopal plant of Union Carbide in India, challenged this logic. In addition, the Exxon Valdez oil spill in Alaska placed issues of pollution in the USA in the public consciousness. Distinct sectors of the business community and non-profit organizations responded to growing public demand for better corporate environmental management with the release of a series of voluntary initiatives, in the form of codes of conduct, environmental guidelines, charters and programmes (Nash & Ehrenfeld, 1997). Self-regulation also appealed as an ethical framework within which companies could represent their actions as responding to public concerns about the safe management of chemicals (King & Lenox, 2000; Prakash, 2000). Similar initiatives, emerging from civil society organizations (CSOs), have also become known as 'civil regulation' (Zadek, 2006). These initiatives share the common objectives of assisting business to implement environmental programmes and communicating them to the general public. Such voluntarism acted to deflect governments from imposing more restrictive regulations. A new mode of regulation started to emerge and a new phase of industry–governments relationship gradually gained ground (Howes, Skea, & Whelan, 1997).

Prakash and Potoski (2006) group such voluntary initiatives under the umbrella title of *Green Clubs*. Such clubs help firms to manage their reputation, especially where their operations have caused reputational damage through accidents or local pollution. By becoming members of Green Clubs corporations presumably will improve their environmental performance. The improvements, however, depend on the constituency of Green Clubs: often, the more demanding clubs were founded by a CSO,[2] which aimed at gathering a wide range of stakeholders. Sector-specific Green Clubs, on the other hand, tend to be initiated by industrial associations with the original aim of protecting members against reputational ill. At least in the early stages, these clubs are inclined to concentrate on legal compliance and cost-cutting exercises, as Responsible Care did for the chemical industry.

The adoption of Green Club doctrines and guidelines may help corporations create positive public opinion about organizational practices. As indicated by Dowel, Hart, and Yeung (2000), for instance, a significant positive relationship between the market value of multinationals and the environmental standards used in their factories worldwide can be identified. Besides being cost effective for firms, the market may also value homogeneous (beyond compliance) standards across plants, reflected in stock values. The reputation of buyer organizations, normally located in wealthy countries, can also be affected by upstream practices throughout the value chain in emerging economies. For this reason responsible operations throughout the value chain became crucial (Christmann & Taylor, 2001). The growing number of certifications from companies operating in developing countries is a consequence of these elaborated value chains (Albuquerque, Bronneberg, & Corbett, 2007).

Overall, the proliferation of Green Clubs with general principles, codes of conduct and behaviour guidelines, will limit business impacts on nature. However, as the expulsion of members that do not comply with the clubs' requirements is a rarity, there is room to question whether the clubs are more window-dressing rather than sources of self-restraining management policy. Indeed, as Orsato (2009) has indicated, these initiatives have served defensive goals very well. In the majority of cases, by endorsing the codes of green clubs, companies have avoided the disadvantages of being exposed to bad reputational campaigns.

In the following sections we focus on the context and historical developments (Sections 3, 4 and 5) that culminated in the foundation of a very large and ambitious Green Club: the RSPO, which has helped to protect the reputation of the industry in the recent past. However, as we elaborate, using the political ecology framework (Section 6), the legitimation of the club and its claims did not occur without major political disputes.

## 3. Palm Oil and Development in Malaysia and Indonesia

The labels of various foodstuffs, cosmetics, soaps, detergents and fuel often state that the product contains 'vegetable oil'. The source of vegetable oil may be from any one or more of 15 or so different plants. Most probably, however, the vegetable in question will be the palm, the resource used in the manufacture of palm oil. The production of 42 million tons (Mt) of palm oil in 2010 means that palm oil now surpasses soybeans (35 Mt) as the most heavily traded agricultural product: indeed, it is the number one commodity in the category of vegetable oil. Due to its high yields – about nine times that of soybeans – palm oil is highly price competitive.

Asia accounts for more than 60% of domestic consumption of palm oil, followed by the European Union (EU) with 10%. In Asia, palm oil is largely used in the production of foodstuffs, personal care items and detergents. In Europe, the statistics demonstrate quite different uses: the EU became the second largest importer of palm oil in 2004, just behind China, almost exclusively on the basis of its use as a biofuel. The reasons for its adoption in this sphere are closely associated with a widespread view of biofuels as 'carbon-neutral'. A growing world population, which will double demand for food by 2050, and increasing economic affluence in developing countries, has intensified the demand for vegetable oils. The estimate for 2050 is that the world crop will be about 240 Mt, roughly twice the current production. Between 1995 and 2008, for instance, growth in demand and the competitive prices of palm oil resulted in the area under cultivation increasing by 43%, while production increased about 2.5 times.

Palm oil production was established in Malaysia to supply European markets in the late nineteenth and early twentieth centuries, being developed on the basis of a plantation economy under the control of global interests established in the core of the world economy, such as Lever Bros. Nevertheless, its major expansion started only in the 1960s as a response to the post-Colonial Malaysian Government's diversification policies. These were designed to reduce the dependence of the national economy on natural rubber, another plantation crop, which faced competition from synthetic rubber and a declining price. In the 1970s, palm oil plantations started to expand into more remote areas such as the Borneo states of Sabah and Sarawak.

The production of palm oil is a labour intensive agricultural activity that was envisaged by government as a means for reducing rural poverty, something encouraged by the creation of the Federal Land Development Agency (FELDA) in 1956. The development process consisted of clearing forests, planting palm trees, settling unemployed people, including ex-soldiers and Bumiputra (ethnic Malays) from elsewhere, as well as installing processing mills and marketing the oil. Although FELDA stopped the intake of new settlers in 1990, in 2002 its settlements accounted for 17% of the planted area and 20.6% of palm oil production in Malaysia.

Agriculture, forestry and fishing have traditionally been the main economic sectors of Malaysia contributing nearly 30% of the economy in 1970, although this had declined to 8.5% by 2007, when these sectors still employed 13% of the population. Overall, despite its strong contribution to the country's development in the past, the Malaysian palm oil industry is at the crossroads. As a mature industry, unless it can achieve further growth and remain competitive, its contribution to the national economy will stagnate and eventually decline. Expansion is, however, limited by the increasing scarcity of two essential inputs – land and labour. Land expansion is restricted by the opposition of environmental activists to the clearing of native forests, while affluence is limiting the availability of people willing to work and live near palm oil farms.

In Indonesia the situation is similar. Palm oil is considered as a strategic commodity for the country not only because it is the main cooking oil for the population but also that oil was a key product that rescued Indonesia during the Southeast Asian Economic Crisis in 1998, when palm oil's price shot up to US$ 600/barrel. Palm oil plantations in Indonesia grew from 5.06 Mha in 2002 to 6.33 Mha in 2006. Riau, a 9 Mha province, has the highest concentration of peat land in the world and a quarter of Indonesia's oil palm plantations. Substantial growth has been achieved but with high environmental impact. According to the

Indonesian Palm Oil Board, in 2006 about 2 million people were employed in the sector, and in 2007 agriculture accounted for 13% of Indonesian GDP, making it one of the largest producers and consumers of agricultural products in Asia.

## 4. Palm Oil and Human Rights

Palm oil production occurs through an intensive plantation economy that has displaced traditional indigenous pursuits of hunter-gathers. Traditional owners are not necessarily recognized in the administration of the palm oil economy.

> The government official asked me if I have a land ownership certificate and I answered that every single durian tree, and every single tengkawang [Shorea spp. – illipe nut trees] tree, and every single rubber tree that we or our ancestors have planted are certificates. I am an indigenous person born here. My ancestors have already defended this land for generations. I do not want outsiders to disturb us. We will not allow any companies to establish plantations on our land. (Indigenous leader, Sekadau District)

After Indonesia's seizure of independence from the Dutch in 1945, when the Japanese occupiers were evicted, a series of laws were enacted making the newly independent state's government a major landowner. As a result, it is estimated that 60–90 million people derive their livelihoods from land classified as 'State Forest Areas', which cover 70% of Indonesia's territory. Many of its rural lands consist of primary and secondary forests, in which there are agro-forestry systems with rotations of 30 years or more, including community planted rubber forests or other cash crops, fruit groves, as well as community-protected sites of cultural significance, such as burial sites in forest groves, in addition to homesteads.

Local communities adjacent to palm oil production are remote and fragmented, in terms of their relations with government and corporations. Unsurprisingly, such asymmetry in power distribution leads to a history of bad practices. Local communities are often impoverished and displaced. Palm oil is labour intensive. Its cultivation in what were previously forestlands that have been cleared means that its expansion takes place in what have become relatively unpopulated or low-population density areas. Recently, community support groups, together with local players, have founded NGOs with a mission of empowering and protecting communities. One such organization is Sawit Watch (palm oil watcher), an Indonesian local NGO supported by Oxfam Novib, was founded in 1998. Sawit Watch contacts and informs communities about their rights in relation to overall power disputes and how they affect their particular locale, as well as providing guidelines for action. At the beginning of 2008, there were 513 active conflicts identified in the 17 provinces (out of 33 provinces in Indonesia) where it had volunteers working.

NGOs have not prevented people from being harassed, abducted, killed, arrested and having their houses burned. Nonetheless, Sawit Watch and other NGOs have reported irregularities such as a lack of community consultation, as required by law; pay-offs of stakeholders and the provision of inflated promises in community consultations; a lack of clear negotiations concerning the allocation of oil palm smallholdings; the clearing of forested land without permits; a reluctance to either achieve or comply with environmental impact assessments; and corruption, especially of local political interests, all of which have led to disputes and conflicts.

## 5. Palm Oil and the Environment

### *5.1 Deforestation*

Besides credit from banks, the main means of expansion of plantations is the sale of timber (both legally and illegally logged). As the production of palm oil is expected to increase, those high conservation value forests remaining are endangered. Between 1990 and 2000, Malaysia and Indonesia lost 25.6% of their forests. Since the late 1990s the rate of deforestation has increased even further in tandem with the scarcity of timber and illegal logging in national parks. The orang-utan habitat loss had increased 30% and, if things continued as they are now, by 2022 the forests in Malaysia and Indonesia will be nearly gone (Nellemann et al., 2007).

### *5.2 Local Pollution*

> In the past, when there was no oil palm plantation here, water in the river was very deep, but now it's very shallow. We run out of water, it is difficult for people to find clean water in the dry season, not everyone has a drilled well. In the past in the forest, after a month and a half of dry season we would still find many small rivers. Nowadays after a month or so of dry season they have all dried up. (Smallholder, West Kalimantan)

The most important impact caused by palm oil production is water pollution. Plantations are intensively sprayed with pesticides and herbicides, creating toxic runoff, while effluent from the milling process is also toxic and, because of this, should be stored in special ponds. Nonetheless, Sawit Watch report that it is common to receive reports of effluents being discharged into rivers. Large palm oil plantations require substantial levels of water, normally supplied by irrigation. As a result, access to water becomes increasingly difficult in some communities. Although oil palm plantations are planted in areas of relatively high rainfall, some communities' report that local rivers now have far less water. The most evident detrimental effect of palm oil plantation can be seen at the end of the life cycle of the plantation economy; plantations are often abandoned due to soil exhaustion after a 25-year cycle (the average time the trees are productive).

### *5.3 Carbon Emissions*

After China and the USA, Indonesia is the third largest emitter of Greenhouse Gas (GHG) in the world, accounting for 4% of global emissions. The emissions from peat lands – drained to plant palm oil – represent 1% of total global emissions. Indeed, around half of the 22 million hectares of peat lands has already been cleared in Indonesia. In 2007, 20% of global GHG emissions came from deforestation and peat land degradation or drainage. Emissions have increased almost

50% since the early 1990s, largely as a direct result of the expansion of oil palm and pulpwood plantations into Indonesia's peat lands. Palm oil produced on peat land with a depth of three metres carries a carbon burden more than 20 times the emissions linked to crude oil.

### *5.4 Biofuels*

> The surging tide of food prices, such as corn, wheat and palm oil, continues to add to the already worsening global inflationary pressure. ( . . . ) The record high crude oil prices further added pressure on the global economy, and heighten the fuel-food debacle. (Tan Sri Dato' Lee Shin Cheng, Executive Chairman at IOI)

Neste, the largest Scandinavian biofuel producer, has positive views on palm oil that are not shared by eco-activist organizations. In May 2007, Greenpeace campaigned in Europe, along with World Wildlife Fund (WWF) and other NGOs, warning the government about the risks of biofuels as an alternative to petrol and diesel. Unilever, a major user of palm oil in cosmetic and other lines (Palmolive soap, for instance), seems to agree. The company declared its concern about biofuels, saying that they are neither environmentally efficient nor cost effective in reducing GHG emissions. According to Unilever, since palm oil is used as cooking oil by two billion of the poorest people in the world, any price increase has direct consequences on their purchasing power. Of course, it also has an impact on their input factor prices

## 6. Circuits of Political Ecology

As we have intimated, the evolution of events in the recent history of the palm oil industry (mainly from 1997 to 2011) has been politically complex. Institutional-power relations, cultural clashes and political economic disputes have all been involved in palm oil's development. We will use the *political ecology framework* (Orsato & Clegg, 1999), originally adapted from Clegg's (1989) circuits of power, to conceptualize the issues. Only as the process unfolds are we able to translate the sense that is being made, which we now represent in Figure 1 and describe in the remaining parts of the paper. In other words, we use the framework to intertwine the data with its interpretation.

### *6.1 Agency: The 1997 Haze*

> People and the media started asking why every year the fires in Malaysia and Indonesia were so bad – it was affecting public health even in Singapore. Part of the answer was palm oil [ . . . ] So, what initiated everything were the fires, a forestry issue, and not the orang-utans. Orang-utans are a sexy subject linked to the issue because preserving the forest is preserving biodiversity. (Teoh Cheng Hai, first RSPO Secretary General)

The haze that engulfed Southeast Asia and spread as far as Australia in 1997 became a key *agency* in the history of the palm oil industry. Large parts of the

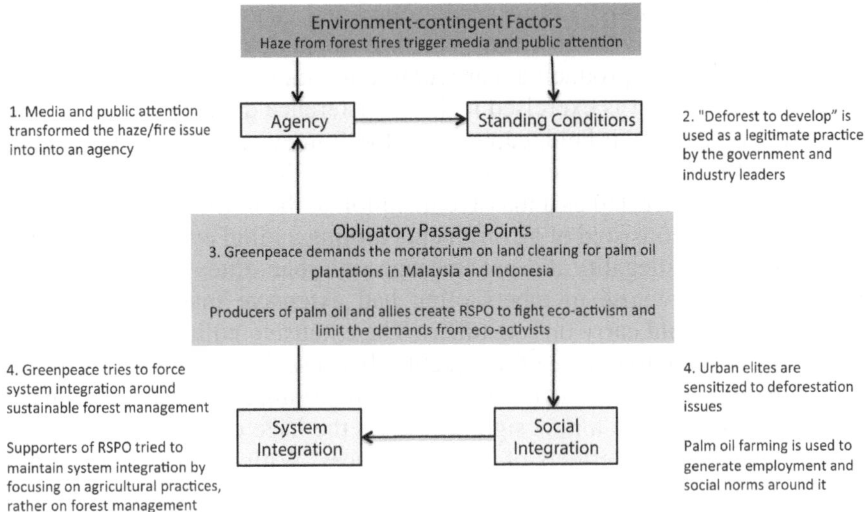


**Figure 1.** Circuits of political ecology in palm oil production.

Indonesian archipelago as well as Singapore and Malaysian cities such as Kuala Lumpur were subject to a thick and unhealthily acrid haze resulting from the burn-off that followed illegal logging, as land was being cleared on a large scale. Prior to this period, urban elites, apart from activists, had not been too concerned about issues of logging and plantation creation that occurred far from their everyday lives. Extensive pollution caused by burning off in the cities changed this situation. During this period of pollution inundating the air that the elites breathed, people (mainly eco-activists and the media) were able to use the extraordinary situation to make others do things that they would not otherwise have done (be concerned about deforestation). The unanticipated effects of the logging and burn-off created an agency – pollution – with the ability to make a difference (Clegg, 1989). The fires started to attract media and public attention because of the direct and indirect environmental impact, which represented a not so clear but very present danger. Indonesia, Malaysia, Singapore, Brunei and Thailand all suffered economic losses, and many people endured health problems from the haze provoked by fires in Borneo. The event received substantial coverage from the media, catching the attention of people in the Australasian region and, over time, the world. Since the fires were set mainly to convert forests into palm oil plantations, for the first time the link between the cultivation of palm oil, deforestation and devastating pollution was clearly established for the general public, creating an important moment for the NGOs that had been campaigning against deforestation and logging in Malaysia and Indonesia.

### *6.2 Standing Conditions: 'Deforest to Develop'*

Agency cannot be exercised independently of the context that maintains and stabilizes the access of agents to resources. We can refer to this context as the set of standing conditions – those background and taken for granted conditions that sustain the stable context within which resource dependence routinely functions as a means for producing particular outcomes. Whether any particular episode in which power is exercised makes a difference depends on the 'systematicity' of the organization field, captured in the framework through the notion of standing conditions. The haze of severe pollution that hung in a pall over the whole region in 1997 acted as a massive irruption to the normalcy of extant standing conditions that consisted of governments turning a blind eye to illegal logging. For as long as this illegality did not impinge on urban elites and their networks then governments, whose members often had extensive interests in industries such as logging, could carry on regardless. The extensive pollution severely compromised the implicit tolerance of urban elites because the results of illegal actions were no longer contained, at a distance, safe from prying eyes. The activism of the eco-campaigners took on a new significance as the haze confirmed the reality of their warnings about the effects of land clearances. With the standing conditions for the normal business of illegal logging and plantation colonization of the cleared spaces disturbed, the power plays of leading actors were both more exposed and compromised.

### *6.3 Institutional Entrepreneurs and Obligatory Passage Points: The Foundation of the RSPO Green Club*

The circuits of power in and around palm oil were transformed by the emergence of a new institutional entrepreneur in the organizational field, the WWF. The term, institutional entrepreneur, was introduced by DiMaggio (1988) when he described institutional entrepreneurship as the activity underlying the creation of new institutions: 'new institutions arise when organized actors with sufficient resources see in them an opportunity to realize interests that they value highly . . . [Institutional entrepreneurs] create a whole new system of meaning that ties the functioning of disparate sets of institutions together' (DiMaggio, 1988, p. 14). Institutional entrepreneurs play a pivotal role in creating or changing institutions (Clemens & Cook, 1999; Fligstein, 1997; Greenwood & Suddaby, 2006).

As a specific mechanism for institutional change, 'institutional entrepreneurship represents the activities of actors who have an interest in particular institutional arrangements and who leverage resources to create new institutions or to transform existing ones' (Maguire, Hardy, & Lawrence, 2004, p. 657). This is exactly what WWF did. In 2002 this eco-activist organization initiated an engagement process with stakeholders of the palm oil value chain. In 2004, the initiative was formalized under the name of 'RSPO', with the objective of opening dialogue between stakeholders so as to promote the production of sustainable palm oil throughout the supply chain. The new institutional order emerged from a realization that the interest representation of the palm oil industry had been relatively rudderless and the industry had suffered reputational damage because of the extensive pollution. The decision was made that there had to be some consciously articulated social integration between producers.

The RSPO was designed to be a platform for stakeholders with differing views and positions in the matter. From the perspective of the NGOs, it was better to be involved in decision-making so that they could contribute to practise rather than merely critiquing from outside and at a distance. From the perspective of the producers, although the NGOs were hardly perceived as natural allies, their participation was important if the credibility of the new standing conditions that they were seeking to establish for the industry were to be stabilized. Hence, oil producers have joined *en masse*, representing 41% of RSPO membership and half of the world's palm oil production. The RSPO became a powerful green club.

From the outset, the highest priority of RSPO was to develop Certification on Sustainable Palm Oil for plantations and millers, which standard was launched in December 2007. The standard was to function as an *obligatory passage point* in the institutionalization of the industry as ecologically accountable. The certification requires evidence of compliance to 8 Principles and 39 practical Criteria – also called 'P&C'. The first RSPO certified batch of palm oil was obtained by United Plantations and shipped in November 2008. One aspect of the standard that is notable is that it does not address the wider issues of peat land exploitation and global warming but focuses only on the integrity of *whatever* is manufactured rather than the consequences of *where* it is manufactured.

### *6.4 Resisting the Terms of Institutionalization: Greenpeace's Campaigns*

Institutions reflect, produce and reproduce power relations (Seo & Creed, 2002; Stinchcombe, 1965, p. 194). These power relations can be thought of in terms of entrenched dominant interests and resistance to these entrenched interests (McAdam & Scott, 2005, p. 17). While entrenched interests may have superior material and network resources to engage in entrepreneurship (Greenwood & Suddaby, 2006), resisters generally have stronger incentives and are subject to fewer institutional constraints from the prior shaping of the field (Clemens & Cook, 1999, p. 452; Rao, Morrill, & Zald, 2000, p. 262).

The participation of international NGOs in the RSPO has been divisive. While WWF, Oxfam Novib, Rainforest Alliance and Conservation International joined, others did not. Friends of the Earth, Wetlands International and Greenpeace opted out and have been leading critics of RSPO activities resisting the terms of the institutional field being stabilized:

> At present, the RSPO scheme does not prohibit palm oil producers from being involved in forest conversion and has no assessment of, or limits on, GHG emissions from the development of oil palm plantations. Furthermore, it has no system to segregate palm oil that meets RSPO criteria from palm oil coming from deforestation including peatland clearance. (Greenpeace)

In November 2007, Greenpeace released a report with the title 'Cooking the Climate', linking carbon emissions from cleared peat lands in Indonesia to the activities of RSPO members. The NGO demanded that all players and government not only stop Indonesian peat land fires by establishing a moratorium on clearing peat land for the plantation of palms for oil (which would save 1.3 Gt of $CO_2$ emissions per year) but also that Indonesia's degraded peat lands should be rehabilitated (which would save 0.5 Gt of $CO_2$ per year). In the same month,

Greenpeace welcomed the declaration of the Swedish petrol giant, OKQ8, that it would abandon plans to use palm oil in their new *Eco20* biodiesel.

Not satisfied with the industry's response, Greenpeace launched another campaign in April 2008, this time targeting Unilever – the multinational food producer. Activists wearing orang-utan costumes protested in front of the corporate headquarters in London and other installations in Europe. A video in a Dove® advertising format was published on *YouTube* (with 861,381 viewers by June 2009 according to the official link) and tens of thousands of emails were sent to Unilever from people around the world via the website of Greenpeace:

> Unilever failed to bring the rapidly expanding palm oil sector under control. It knows what is going on and nothing is done about kicking out these companies from the Roundtable. (John Sauven, Greenpeace UK executive director)

Greenpeace demanded three things from Unilever: (i) support a moratorium on forest clearance and peat land degradation; (ii) do not trade with those engaged in deforestation and peat land degradation; and (iii) inform suppliers that purchasers will no longer buy from companies engaged in forest conversion and peat land degradation.

Unilever quickly responded to Greenpeace and the general public whose support had been enrolled by their *Cooking the Climate* report, by saying that Unilver shared the same concerns as everyone else about the expansion of palm oil production. Regarding Greenpeace's demands, Unilever said that it: (i) wants to support the moratorium once 'there is ample un-forested land available to meet even the most optimistic estimate of demand' but still acknowledged that there is also work to be done, for which the company does not have the expertise; (ii) prefers to work with suppliers and help them to stop using unsustainable agricultural methods, as it did in the fish and tea industries, and (iii) intends to have all palm oil certified sustainable by 2015.

Unilever's Director at the time tried to convince other stakeholders to engage in the moratorium but only managed to infuriate the palm oil producers.

> We had to face a large opposition that felt completely damaged. Growers come from very far and the moratorium sounded like RSPO certification was not enough. Our suppliers were already asking time to get used to the certification and the support on the moratorium was an extra work. Some of them said 'you are basically saying that we can't grow'. (Lettemieke Mulder, Director of Global External Affairs at Unilever)

The central issue of contestation in the palm oil arena was crystallizing as who should be able to define what should be done in relation to the value chain of palm oil. While the potential Unilever/Greenpeace alliance sought to stabilize a new legitimacy the more traditionally minded and less cosmopolitan palm oil producers were striving to maintain a situation whose legitimacy, in the eyes of global sophisticated urban élites, was already deeply compromised. Positions were defined and represented in concert at national and international levels representing an agreed position from the palm oil plantation industry. The producers sought to structure the emergent circuitry of power on the peat land issues as non-problematic in order to maintain their existing interests (see Event 3 in Figure 1).

### *6.5 System and Social Integration: Still Unstable*

For Lockwood (1964, p. 251), the 'materiality' of any social ordering is evident in the social reality surrounding it. The material conditions of any such ordering include the technological means of control over the physical and social environment as well as the skills associated with them, constituting the basis for *system integration*. *Social integration*, on the other hand, deals with the symbolic sphere, with relations of meaning and the ways in which these define certain types of membership categories in relation to other categories within organizational fields. Hence, social and system integrations are distinct facets of the same 'reality'. Struggles over relations of meaning and membership create social change through changes in social integration. They redefine what it means to be a member of an organizational field as well as what are normal practices within the contexts in which organizations are embedded.

The entry of Greenpeace's *Cooking the Climate* into the arena of palm oil politics destabilized the attempt to create a new institutional legitimacy through certified system integration. The polarized views between industry representatives and NGOs can be observed in the following statement:

> Some of these detractors [from anyone's success] are in form of NGOs who want to relate us [palm oil industry] to forest destruction and habitat loss, and things like that. If you look at the Malaysian palm oil statistics, whatever we have done is all about switching from rubber, coconut or rice to palm oil. It's got nothing to do with habitat loss or destruction, and that's how ignorant these people are. These NGOs are very short-sighted and focused on trying to destroy a good economy like what we have developed out of palm oil. (Tan Sri Datuk Dr Yusof Basiron, CEO of MPOC)

At present this is where things stand. Institutionalization of producer interests has not brought the legitimacy desired; the system integration of the organization field has been achieved but it has not created overall social integration. There is evident tension attached to the participation of Unilever who might yet secede under pressure from Greenpeace.

## 7. Conclusion

In this paper, we used the framework proposed by Orsato and Clegg (1999) for the analysis of a specific business–environment relationship issue. Although voluntary actions of corporate environmental management can partially explain the evolution processes of the greening of industries, it seems imperative to look at business–environment relationships from perspectives that consider the ways in which power relations configure and define an organizational field. The concepts embedded in the framework are not tentative elaborations dissociated from more substantive works on power (see also Flyvbjerg, 1998; Haugaard, 1998). Rather, they represent a long trajectory initiated in the studies of Clegg (1975) that, more recently, have been developed as a specific application of a power perspective for the analysis of business–environment relationships (Orsato & Clegg, 1999; Orsato, den Hond, & Clegg, 2002). Therefore, the paper uses a theoretically grounded framework for the analysis of the political context in which environmental disputes occur – in this case, the organizational field of the palm oil.

The dispute that occurred between Greenpeace and RSPO – the green club formed around the palm oil industry – shows that political actors try to secure their interests through the designation of what is obligatory and what is not in a specific institutional field. In the end, the palm oil manufacturing industry was able to form a sufficiently strong lobby to counteract the demands from Greenpeace, which allowed the industry to reproduce their preferred rules and, with minimal concessions, to approve their own code of conduct and definition of what consists sustainable palm oil. The detailed analysis of such dispute reflects the *political ecology of the palm oil production*, which addresses one of the main criticisms of approaches to environmental issues in organization studies: that more political perspectives are necessary (Jermier, Forbes, Benn, & Orsato, 2006).

We used the institutional field as the basic level of analysis in our study, which encompasses relations that are usually conceptualized as occurring within the traditional notion of an industrial sector. In doing so, we also satisfy the need for more studies developed at this level of analysis, as proposed by Hoffman (1999), in which the definition of the 'field' is based on the development of 'an issue'. In this respect, our study of the 'palm oil issue' has implications for the development of an important theoretical tradition – institutionalism in sociological and organizational theory.

The institutional tradition has been criticized for neglecting the role of the state and of power relations in its theorizing (Clegg, 2010), an omission that we have sought to redress in this paper. We have explicitly married a field-level institutional analysis to a well-founded and legitimated theoretical framework drawn from the power literature. Doing this has enabled us to draw conclusions that go beyond stressing the usual role of institutional entrepreneurship in creating a new field. In fact, while stressing such entrepreneurship, we show that the field being constructed remains a contested terrain. In so doing, we do not fall prey to the problems of over-institutionalized analysis which sees normative coherence and isomorphism as a characteristic of the institutional field. By contrast, we argue that institutional fields can remain dynamic and unstable and the creation of a new institutional logic – such as that of RSPO – does not necessarily create isomorphic dominance and stability.

Finally, our study indicated that isomorphism emerges from conflict and negotiation over meaning and membership occurring in the organizational field. In this respect, it corroborates the findings of King and Lenox (2000, p. 698), which stresses 'the potential for opportunism to overcome the isomorphic pressures of even self-regulatory institutions and suggest that industry self-regulation is difficult to maintain without explicit sanctions'. Our own findings also suggest that the actions of the Green Club of palm oil producers in moving towards certification to increase legitimacy should be balanced by consideration of the overall dynamics of the political ecology. Although palm oil producers did indeed work to secure their interests, they succeeded only temporarily in maintaining the elements of political ecology unaltered because other players within the overall circuitry – invisible to the producers before the haze of 1997 ignited urban elites – mainly eco-activist organizations, have also been forcing transformation. What was once a fairly local set of circuits has become globally constituted in circuits of political ecology that are far from stable in the now dynamic and global institutional field.

## Notes

1. We collected secondary data from several sources, including media releases, websites of associations and producers, newspaper articles and articles published over the Internet. We also collected data and perspectives about the industry during the Workshop on the Oil Palm Controversy in Transnational Perspective in Singapore in late 2009.

   In order to have a preliminary understanding of the industry and identify key players, we performed phone interviews with Dr Uwe Schulte (former Global Supply Chain Director at Unilever) and Lettemieke Mulder (Director of Global External Affairs, Corporate Responsibility and NGO Stakeholder Management at Unilever).

   The collection of primary data involved interviews in Singapore with Kaisa Hietala (Commercial Director of Neste Oil Singapore), Norman Jiwan (Head of Social and Environmental Risk Mitigation at Sawit Watch), Dato'Mamat Salleh (CEO at MPOA) and Darrel Webber (WWF) and in Kuala Lumpur Malaysia with Puvan J. Selvanathan (Group Chief Sustainability Officer at Sime Darby), M. R. Chandran (RSPO executive board advisor) and Cheng Hai (First Secretary, RSPO).We also spent a week visiting palm oil plantations in the island of Borneo in May 2009. Besides informal conversations with local workers and villagers, we interviewed Jeremy Goon (head of CSR at Wilmar) and the team from Sabahmas plantation.

2. In the paper, we adopted the concept of CSO proposed by the UN Global Compact: Civil society organizations – also known as non-governmental organizations (NGOs) – are critical actors in the advancement of universal values around human rights, the environment, labour standards and anti-corruption. As global market integration has advanced, their role has gained particular importance in aligning economic activities with social and environmental priorities.

## References


Albuquerque, P., Bronneberg, B., & Corbett, C. (2007). A spaciotemporal analysis of the global diffusion of ISO 9000 and 14000 certification. *Management Science, 53*(3), 451–468.

Antweiller, W., Copeland, B. R., & Taylor, M. S. (2001). Is free trade good for the environment? *American Economic Review, 91*(4), 877–908.

Borck, J. C., & Coglianese, C. (2009). Voluntary environmental programs: Assessing their effectiveness. *Annual Review of Environment and Resources, 34*, 305–324.

Christmann, P., & Taylor, G. (2001). Globalization and the environment: Strategies for international voluntary environmental initiatives. *Academy of Management Executive, 16*(3), 121–135.

Clegg, S. R. (1975). *Power, rule and domination*. London: Routledge.

Clegg, S. R. (1989). *Frameworks of power*. London: Sage.

Clegg, S. R. (2010). The state, power and agency: Missing in action in institutional theory? *Journal of Management Inquiry, 19*(1), 4–13.

Clemens, E. S., & Cook, J. M. (1999). Politics and institutionalism: Explaining durability and change. *Annual Review of Sociology, 25*(1), 441–466.

DiMaggio, P. (1988). Interest and agency in institutional theory. In L. G. Zucker (Ed.), *Institutional patterns and organizations: Culture and environment* (pp. 3–21). Cambridge, MA: Ballinger.

DiMaggio, P., & Powell, W. (1983). The iron cage revisited: Institutional isomorphism and collective rationality in organisational fields. *American Sociological Review, 48*, 147–160.

Dowel, G., Hart, S., & Yeung, B. (2000). Do corporate global environmental standards create or destroy value? *Management Science, 46*(8), 1059–1074.

Fiorino, D. (2006). *The new environmental regulation*. Cambridge, MA: MIT Press.

Fligstein, N. (1997). Social skill and institutional theory. *American Behavioral Scientist, 40*(4), 397–405.

Flyvbjerg, B. (1998). *Rationality and power: Democracy in practice*. Chicago, IL: University of Chicago Press.

Greenwood, R., & Suddaby, R. (2006). Institutional entrepreneurship in mature fields: The Big Five accounting firms. *Academy of Management Journal, 49*(1), 27–48.

Haugaard, M. (1998). *The constitution of power*. Manchester: Manchester University Press.

Hoffman, A. J. (1999). Institutional evolution and change: Environmentalism and the U.S. chemical industry. *Academy of Management Journal, 42*(4), 351–371.

Hoffman, A. J. (2001). Linking organizational and field-level analysis. *Organization & Environment, 14*(2), 133–156.

Howes, R., Skea, J., & Whelan, B. (1997). *Clean and competitive? Motivating environmental performance in industry*. London: Earthscan.

Jermier, J., Forbes, L., Benn, S., & Orsato, R. J. (2006). The new corporate environmentalism and green politics. In S. Clegg, C. Hardy, T. Lawrence, & W. Nord (Eds.), *Handbook of organization studies* (2nd ed., pp. 618–650). London: Sage.

King, A. A., & Lenox, M. J. (2000). Industry self-regulation without sanctions: The chemical industry's responsible care program. *The Academy of Management Journal, 43*(4), 698–716.

King, A. A., Lenox, M. J., & Terlaack, A. (2005). The strategic use of decentralized institutions: Exploring certification with the ISO 14001 management standard. *Academy of Management Journal, 46*(6), 1091–1106.

Lockwood, D. (1964). Social integration and system integration. In G. K. Zollschorn & W. Hirsch (Eds.), *Explorations in social change* (pp. 244–257). London: Routledge.

Maguire, S., Hardy, C., & Lawrence, T. B. (2004). Institutional entrepreneurship in emerging fields: HIV/AIDS treatment advocacy in Canada. *Academy of Management Journal, 47*(5), 657–679.

McAdam, D., & Scott, R. W. (2005). Organizations and movements. In G. Davis, D. McAdam, R. Scott, & M. Zald (Eds.), *Social movements and organization theory* (pp. 4–40). Cambridge: Cambridge University Press.

Nash, J., & Ehrenfeld, J. (1997). Codes of environmental management practice: Assessing their potential as a tool for change. *Annual Review of Energy and the Environment, 22*, 487–535.

Orsato, R. (2009). *Sustainability strategies: When does it pay to be green?* London: Palgrave McMillan.

Orsato, R. J., & Clegg, S. R. (1999). The political ecology of organisations: Framing environment-competitiveness relationships. *Organization & Environment, 12*(3), 263–289.

Orsato, R. J., den Hond, F., & Clegg, S. (2002). The political ecology of automobile recycling in Europe. *Organization Studies Journal, 23*(4), 639–665.

Prakash, A. (2000). Responsible care: An assessment. *Business & Society, 39*(2), 183–209.

Prakash, A., & Potoski, M. (2006). Racing to the bottom? Globalization, environmental governance, and ISO 14001. *American Journal of Political Science, 50*(2), 347–361.

Prakash, A., & Potoski, M. (2012). Voluntary environmental programs: A comparative perspective. *Journal of Policy Analysis and Management, 31*(1), 123–238.

Rao, H., Morrill, C., & Zald, M. N. (2000). Power plays: How social movements and collective action create new organizational forms. *Research in Organizational Behaviour, 22*, 239–282.

Seo, M.-G., & Creed, W. E. D. (2002). Institutional contradictions, praxis and institutional change: A dialectical perspective. *Academy of Management Review, 27*(3), 222–247.

Stinchcombe, A. L. (1965). Social structure and organizations. In J. G. March (Ed.), *Handbook of organizations* (pp. 142–193). Chicago, IL: Rand McNally.

UNEP & UNESCO. (2007). *The last stand of the orangutan, 2007. State of emergency: Illegal logging, fire and palm oil in Indonesia's National Parks*. Retrieved from https://ia600507.us.archive.org/10/items/laststandoforang07nell/laststandoforang07nell.pdf.

Vogel, D. (2006). *The market for virtue. The potential and limits of corporate social responsibility*. Washington, DC: Brooking Institution Press.

White, H. (1992). *Identity and control: A structural theory of social integration*. Princeton, NJ: Princeton University Press.

Zadek, S. (2006). *The civil corporation: The new economy of corporate citizenship*. London: Earthscan.

# From the Physics of Change to Realpolitik: Improvisational Relations of Power and Resistance

MIGUEL PINA E CUNHA*, STEWART R. CLEGG*,**,
ARMÉNIO REGO†,‡ & JOANA STORY*

*Nova School of Business and Economics, Lisboa, Portugal, **Faculty of Business, University of Technology, Sydney, Australia, †Departamento de Economia, Gestão e Engenharia Industrial, Universidade de Aveiro, Portugal, ‡UNIDE, Instituto Universitário de Lisboa (ISCTE-IUL), Portugal

ABSTRACT *Change and resistance to change constitute a long-lasting couple in the organizational literature. We problematize the mechanistic action-reaction types of analyses, uncover some fragilities in the current debates, and offer minimal structures and the improvisations they favour as possibilities for reconsidering the roles attached to the participants in change processes beyond the established separation between agents and recipients. Improvisation is a space where the established orders of organizing are challenged and alternative orders are allowed to flourish. We suggest that structural interventions, such as minimizing structure, shifting roles and combining paradoxical requirements, help to diffuse resistance to change and to recreate the nature of change in organizations.*

## Introduction

With this paper we rejoin the debate on the reframing of resistance to change (e.g. Dent & Goldberg, 1999; Piderit, 2000). Sustainable change management is often presented in terms of management's decisions to do some new things that improve the green credentials and image of a company. Think of an organization such as British Petroleum (BP) that morphed into bp (beyond petroleum). Globally their petrol stations reflect the green ethos that they transmit in their advertising and branding. Practically, however, in the wake of the *Deepwater Horizon* oil spill in the Gulf of Mexico on the BP-operated Macondo Prospect, which is considered as the largest accidental marine oil spill in the history of the petroleum industry, these representations are in tatters. When image and practice collide corporate representations can expect to take a hammering, especially when they become subject to forensic investigation in court. In the court proceedings launched by the justice Department in New Orleans prosecutors will seek to prove that gross negligence caused the 20 April 2010 blast that killed 11 workers and sank the BP-leased Deepwater Horizon rig, gushing millions of barrels of oil into the sea.

> The US government plans to introduce ample evidence of 'systemic problems of corporate recklessness' and how a 'culture of disregard to safety' led to the blowout, said Michael Underhill, lead trial counsel for the United States. 'Reckless actions were tolerated, sometimes encouraged by BP to squeeze every dollar', he told the court. BP is hoping to shift much of the blame – and cost – to rig operator Transocean and subcontractor Halliburton, which was responsible for the runaway well's faulty cement job. (Miller, 2013)

BP is using a classic strategy of denying responsibility for its management.[1] It is arguing that it had designed sound systems but that it was the resistance of those charged with their implementation to carrying out the designed management system that caused the spill. In other words, they managed responsibly but the subcontracted agencies resisted.

The idea that change is designed at the top and then implemented at the base is problematic for at least two reasons. First, it establishes a separation between thinking and action. Second, it does not overcome a separation that has stubbornly remained at the core of management since the inception of the discipline: the need for change and its correlate, resistance to change (Coch & French, 1948; Lawrence, 1954; Lewin, 1947). Resistance to change is usually defined as 'a form of dissent to a change process (or series of practices) that the individual considers unpleasant, disagreeable or inconvenient on the basis of personal or group evaluations' (Giangreco & Peccei, 2005, pp. 1816–1817). These two core antagonisms reveal an interesting and paradoxical question: why do organizations persist in striving for change that their members so resist? Or, to put another way, why do managers' 'good intentions' produce so many 'failed implementations'? (Danisman, 2010)

If 'change' is presented to its 'recipients' as a packaged black box or what Follett termed as 'finished plans' (Graham, 1995, p. 220), violating the three basic principles of fair process (engagement, explanation and expectation clarity; Kim & Mauborgne, 2005), then it seems unsurprising that recipients will not adhere enthusiastically to its implementation and will boycott, both passively or actively, the change implementation. The 'packaged' perspective simplifies a number of dimensions of organizational life, including constituting the role of employees as apathetic executants of orders from on high; it mistakes the role of emergence as a nuisance to be avoided rather than as a property of complex systems and it is blank in the face of the power dynamics that are constitutive of organizations (ironically, given the central role of such packaging in these).

Through a self-fulfilling prophecy (Ford, Ford, & D'Amelio, 2008), change agents also and invariably act as resistance agents, which is why from a managerial perspective resistance should be viewed as a form of feedback, a communicative resource (Ford & Ford, 2009) and an expression of organizing.

First, we problematize the idea that change management is a process that only managers do. Second, we problematize the idea that resistance to change is a practice that only employees adopt. Third, we expose a paradox of change: why do people resist? We discuss, in particular, the role of improvisation in the development of self-sustaining change processes throughout the organization. Improvisation as thinking while acting can bridge the seemingly inseparable processes of managerial power relations and employee resistance relations. Finally, we present improvisation as a process that may contribute, within the context of semi-structures, to depart from the dualisms of change towards a duality view by shifting roles and perspectives.

### Introducing Change: Managerial Responsibility?

The assumption underlying most research on change work is that change is a process that managers manage and which their employees frequently resist (Dent & Goldberg, 1999), change referring to 'the process by which organizations alter their structure, strategy, technology, culture, or systems and the outcomes of the process' (Ocasio, 2008, p. 1020). Consider the following explanation:

> A central debate in the strategy, organizations, and entrepreneurship literatures surrounds how *leaders* effectively manage their organizations and strategies in dynamic environments. (Eisenhardt, Furr, & Bingham, 2010, p. 1263, i.a.)

Note that in the quotation *leaders* are said to manage their organizations' adaptive efforts. The focus on leaders is recurrent in Eisenhardt and her colleagues' analysis: 'how leaders balance efficiency and flexibility within organizations', 'how leaders actively manage the tension between efficiency and flexibility through cognitively sophisticated single solutions' and 'how leaders effectively manage the fundamental tension between efficiency and flexibility in dynamic environments' (p. 1265). The insistence on how *leaders* accomplish adaptation suggests a romance of leadership (Meindl, Ehrlich, & Dukerich, 1985). While leaders may be influential they are not *the organization*. Reducing the organization to the leader represents a simplification that obscures the role of followers, relationships, networks, habits, processes and superstitions in the change process. If we equate, as is often the case, change management with the way *leaders* attempt to manage change, the seeds of resistance will already be planted because executive vision is being privileged over all other definitions of the situation. Unless a great deal of negotiation and compromise has already occurred, the realization that different people see things differently will be lost (Kim & Mauborgne, 2005). We do not deny the role of leaders in the strategic processes, but rather suggest that *organizations* better manage adaptation via co-creation by several stakeholders, including leaders, managers and employees. Seeing change as a process of co-creation differs radically from viewing it as purely as an executive function.

We challenge the dominant view in three ways: (1) against the idea that change is difficult we propose that change is inevitable, (2) against the idea that leaders manage change we argue that organizations produce changes and (3) against the view that change exists because of management we suggest that change does not have to be managed to unfold and that, in some cases, management may be a major barrier against change.

### *Change Is the Natural State – Therefore It Is Inevitable*

Organizations have traditionally been viewed as inertial, hence the need to stimulate change. The reasoning is clear: if change is not induced top-down, organizations will be at rest. The dominance of the concept of equilibrium, central to neo-classical economics, has become widely accepted. Given equilibrium, if things are to change it is usually argued that the changes should be strategic, should be produced at the top and then pushed to the base.

A dominant management conceptualization proposes 'periods of social change may differ quite markedly from periods of relative social stability' (Lewin, 1947, p. 13). However, as Lewin also remarked, the two concepts exist in a dialectic relationship: 'Any formula which states the conditions for change implies the conditions for no-change' (p. 13). It was the popularity of change conceived as a rational process entailing the succession of three steps ('unfreezing, moving and freezing'; Lewin, 1947, p. 34) that led to the separation view. In this model, when managers do not unfreeze the status quo, the organization stays still. The axiom persists in multiple forms. For example, in Kotter's (1996) well-known model, change starts with the creation of a sense of urgency. If change is not perceived as urgent, it will be resisted. Change managers are agents of disequilibrium: they destabilize the system to make change possible. Normal organization comes to be regarded as a land of stasis in which routines merely repeat themselves.

Against the stasis of equilibrium models, diverse intellectual and artistic traditions suggest a more historically dynamic view of change as a permanent unfolding. Ancient philosophers, such as Heraclitus, poets, such as the sixteenth-century poet Camoes, as well as process organization scholars all indicate change to be the natural state. Camoes said it poetically: 'all the world is made of change/always gaining new qualities' and complexity theorists elaborated the point in prose, noting that complex systems are 'interactions among many dynamic degrees of freedom, the outcome of which cannot be predicted' (Marion & Uhl-Bien, 2011, p. 386). In a complexity perspective, organization becomes seen as a property of change, rather than change being a property of organization – the other way around (Tsoukas, 2005). As Kerber and Buono (2005, p. 27) observed, 'continuous *change is* a *natural* part of organizational life', suggesting that 'it is increasingly common for change to arise from all levels in the organization, for people to make both small and large changes in their work based on trial and error and success and failure and for changes initiated in one part of an organization to spread to other parts of the company'. In short, change is the normal state of affairs and resisting it should be understood as a constitutive part of the dynamics of this normalcy (Courpasson, Dany, & Clegg, 2012).

### *Change as an* Organizational *Process*

Our second point refers to the locus of change. Consider the unfolding data relating the fall of various dictatorial regimes in the Middle East, such as Gadhafi's. Change was not managed by leaders but by resisters. Change and resistance may better be viewed as processes immanent to and products of organizing, a process that unfolds irrespective of the presence of managers who may wish to direct or constrain it. Reducing change to the work of 'change masters' while neglecting the role of change that is grassroots, organic and managerially illegitimate is a simplification that presumes an appearance, apparatus and activity of control where it is often revealed to be illusory. We argue that change is a process that organizations do – not (only) leaders. The point may sound evident, but the assumption of the primacy of leaders is obvious: it is managers that *manage* change. Change is not what happens to them.

Change is something that organizations produce while they attempt to organize. The inherent humanity and instability of organizing fuels change whether managers like it or not. As Tsoukas and Chia (2002, p. 568) observed:

> insofar as routines are performed by human agents, they contain the seeds of change. In other words, even the most allegedly stable parts of organizations, such as routines, are potentially unstable. Change is always potentially there if we only care to look for it.

In this formulation, focusing just on managers to understand change means that the places where the micro-processes of change will have to be made, where it will happen, will be ignored; resistance as an integral and everyday phenomena will be stigmatized.

### *Change Need Not Be Managed to Take Place*

Change need not be managed or sanctioned to unfold. Even radical change may be created in the absence of intention, as a result of interactive dynamics (Plowman et al., 2007). In other words, it does not take management to trigger complex, even radical, change processes. As we have noted, collective movements such as the Jasmin revolutions in North Africa were not produced because of management: they were actually produced *against* management. They resulted from the combination of a number of factors that produced a radical unplanned outcome. In the process some people eventually assumed leadership roles but leadership was a creation of change, not the other way around. As the ongoing Arabic struggles indicate, sometimes leaders are the obstacles to change. The implications of this point are clear: (a) organizations may not need managers to initiate change, (b) sometimes managers are impediments to change and (c) complex systems produce changes that cannot be planned or, strictly speaking, led.

**Resisting Change: Employee Response?**

In the previous section we suggested that change is not necessarily a process whose responsibility is assigned to managers. In this one, we suggest that employees do not necessarily initiate resistance. Resistance can be co-produced by leaders and the led.

*Change and Resistance Are Co-Produced*

Resistance is often presented as a counter-force exerted by employees to limit the intentions of managers, in which terms it is defined as 'those organizational activities and attitudes that aim to thwart, undermine and impede change initiatives' (Fleming, 2008, p. 1376). The reasons for this counter-power are many, including a defence of class and/or individual interest (Clegg & Dunkerley, 1980), the pleasure of resisting (Deetz, 2008), dispositional resistance (Oreg, Vakola, & Armenakis, 2011) and the translation (and sometimes, from an elite perspective, the degradation) of a change message as it travels through the organization (Kurke, Weick, & Ravlin, 1989). Regardless of the motive, the responsibility for resistance as traditionally represented is clear: it is employees who are the ones resisting.

The representation caricatures the process: resistance is dialectical, a relationship, the result of interactions, of contests over meaning and action (Courpasson et al., 2012; Kahn, 2011). It is co-produced and co-constitutive (Thomas & Hardy, 2011). Employees are not passively waiting for a change initiative to boycott it when it arrives. Rather, change is produced and resisted on an ongoing basis. Organizations are configurations that sustain and are sustained by an existing power circuitry, which, in turn, emergently establishes those changes that are created and those that are neutralized or amplified (Clegg, 1989). Power circuits conduct change energies in such a way that they influence the outcomes of change processes, 'judging' which change initiatives are accomplished and those that will not. For example, some years ago, *The Guardian* reported (Ward, 2005) that 'flexible working has boomed in UK workplaces over the past three years but its growth is still hampered by many managers' resistance to change', one reason being managers' concerns/fears of not seeing people 'sat at their desks nearby'.

Most realistic managers will manage what they can manage and resist what will potentially destroy their positions in power networks. That is why it is said that new governments should introduce hard measures before they get to know the functioning of state institutions in any great detail. After that time, they know too much to even start some changes better made from relative ignorance.

*Resistance to Change Is Performative Rather than Reactive*

Countering change requires significant effort and energy, exposing resisters to risks of various sorts. In fact, neutralizing a process that is emergent, spontaneous and sometimes desired by top managers requires volition, organization and determination. Managers use their fiat to try and break the status quo and employees organize themselves formally or informally to counter this fiat. The result is that the process of resistance itself is carefully negotiated and choreographed. Resistance is a dance between employees and managers, not a force imposed over some dormant physical object.

Because change is about politics rather than physics, every move from one party will be invested with symbolism and political meaning (not only to the other party but also among peers; change is destabilizing for all). Change-related behaviours become performative, presenting change as a form of performing art. When organizations seek to 'freeze', in doing so, they express some more or less explicit agreement between the parties. Routines, once achieved, provide a politically safe space for the internal powers.

### *Resistance Is Managed*

Resistance is itself a sophisticated process of (anti-)change management. It mirrors the difficulties and the troubles of starting change from above. Additionally, it requires extra care, for resistance lacks the assumption of formal legitimacy that behooves managerial decisions. Starting change is a need while resisting it requires careful explanation and political skills in challenging existing power balances. In some cases, it should be done only undercover or with a penchant for irony (Fleming & Sewell, 2002).

Resistance, in summary, is management by other means. The twist in this conceptualization of the change/resistance dialectic is that it trades places between what seems spontaneous and what appears as managed. It offers a picture of resistance as a process that is as managed as the process of change. That is, perhaps, why change management seems itself so difficult: it is a process countering a process that, due to its subversive nature, is at least as sophisticated as itself. Because complexity requires complexity (Weick, 1979), resistance must be as complex as change, a possibility that might just explain why change programmes often do not produce change (Beer, Eisenstat, & Spector, 1990).

## The Paradox: Resisting a Process We Need

Change management represents a paradox: why do organizations' managers promote change and simultaneously think it is their prerogative while organization's members resist change, with management maintaining the fiction that any here and now equilibrium is always illusory? This paradox has been noticed and elaborated by several researchers, recently by Nasim and Sushil (2011). Our contribution to this debate resides in the observation that the change can be represented as two fundamentally contradictory sub-processes. In most cases, these two sub-processes will clash given their antithetical nature: macro-change (top-down, planned and led) and micro-change (local, event-driven and improvised). When the contradictions between these two processes are not addressed, dynamic and unsettling power relations will endure and possibly be accentuated. Why then do organizations resist resolution? Several explanations can be advanced.

*Organization for Completeness Produces Resistance*

To organize means reducing variation and introducing stability and predictability. Organization repeats processes that produce an outcome that, locally, can be defined as 'effectiveness', in terms of situated knowledge and norms. Once locally defined effectiveness is achieved, the space for executive change consists only of what, rhetorically, will be taken to increases efficiency: doing the same with less or the process known as exploitation (March, 1991). Such local knowledge too often screens out external contingencies and realities: the problem with this local focus, of course, lies in what is excluded: because change is the natural state, growing organizational efficiency may be a problem in a relentlessly changing world. Even when they are aware of this, organizations may not be able to break existing routines. Substituting the old may be difficult even when signs that it is not working abound. Routines have a history of their own, which result from cycles of negotiation and renegotiation, offers and counter-offers, amongst all the participants engaging in the process, becoming the symbolic focal point of local attention and sensemaking. Once different negotiators reach an agreement, substituting another for it may be difficult, and this difficulty may be reinforced or facilitated of facilitated by some features of organizational culture (Danisman, 2010). In this sense, resistance results are not just from recipients of change resisting but also from organizational path dependencies: the more routinized the organizational design (and its corresponding organizational culture), the more it becomes potentially less receptive to change. Because organization designs so often strive for completeness in terms of management control (Garud, Jain, & Tuertscher, 2008), it should come as no surprise that resistance became so prevalent.

*Resistance Produces More Resistance*

Once inertia sets in, organizations get locked in to the routines that worked in the past. The ghosts of organizational pasts haunt organizational presents, stalking managers with diverse spectre that weigh heavy as a nightmare on the brains of those living to manage (Miller, 1990). As organizations grow and get old, they formalize more in their structural drift towards efficiency (Sorenson & Stuart, 2000). As memories of the past create entrenched identities, challenging old ways becomes a contest over identity rather than a mere 'technicality'. In this sense, to see resistance to change as evidence of a stubborn lack of adherence to new positive possibilities is a trivialization of the process of change management (Dobosz-Bourne & Jankowicz, 2006).

Trivialization of change management means that the positions of the parties involved become progressively locked into the wars of position that separate those agents and recipients. The more people see this opposition as established, the more assumptions confirm reality (Ford et al., 2008). The result is the creation of organizational identities around opposition: initiators align themselves with progress while resisters are described as obstinate conservatives. In a curious inversion, managers become the revolutionaries and workers the reactionaries. A vicious cycle establishes that resistance breeds more resistance in the direction of progressive ossification (Stacey, 1991) around established habits and routines. What makes organizations recognizable over time is also what breaks them in the long run.

### *Cycles of Resistance Make Management Necessary – but Possibly Insufficient – to Produce Change*

When organizations get caught in the trap of simplicity (Miller, 1990), they have a hard time trying to introduce significant change. Change becomes difficult as a result of established identities (Dobosz-Bourne & Jankowicz, 2006). Changing configurations of meanings may be difficult because the memories of past contests over change may reduce the motivation for further change. Freezing tried and tested routines may be distinctly labelled as resistance to change, but it can also be regarded as 'inertia', 'ossification', routinization, stability and identity.

Given the pervasiveness of 'completed' organizational designs that counter change attempts, a significant body of work in the organization and management disciplines has been recently dedicated to the exploration of forms that may support change. Eisenhardt et al. (2010) indicated two possibilities: ambidexterity and semi-structures. Ambidexterity refers to the separation of functions that have to do with stability and change (O'Reilly, Harreld, & Tushman, 2009). In this design, parts of the organization explore while others exploit. Ambidextrous designs provide a number of opportunities for firms as both efficiency-driven machines and flexibility-oriented organisms.

The problem with this form is that it may risk creating 'schizophrenic' approaches that do not easily communicate. Temporal or functional differentiation (Nickerson & Zenger, 2002) can bring invaluable benefits but it does not resolve the change vs. resistance debate: parts of the organization are designed to resist change while others are innovation-driven. Ambidexterity is a potential solution, but still an either/or solution. The real challenge for many organizations is not how to separate spaces for flexibility and for efficiency but how to create designs that accommodate opposite demands such as flexibility and efficiency, change and resistance to change, respect for the past and curiosity for the future.

The resolution of this dilemma typically resides in recognition of so-called semi-structures. Semi-structures are minimal organizational designs that prescribe a limited number of rules. The minimal approach allows a synthesis of order/direction and freedom/adaptability. Semi-structures are design heuristics that result from experiential learning and that, once established, offer simple rules for organizing (Bingham & Eisenhardt, 2011; Brown & Eisenhardt, 1997). Simple rules create combinations of structure and freedom that facilitate improvisation by empowering people for change: the space to experiment, coupled with simple rules that offer the necessary coordination, creates organizing processes marked both by direction and zones for manoeuvring organizational change. The minimalism of semi-structuring dissolves the tension between initiators and recipients by turning every organizational member into a potential initiator *and* a recipient of change. In this logic, organizational *change* initiatives, episodic, general and top-down give way to *changing* processes, ongoing, mundane and local. Minimalism and improvisation dissolve the dualism into a duality (Farjoun, 2010) that defuses the initiation/resistance tension. Speaking about initiators and recipients in the context of semi-structures is meaningless because every organizational member potentially starts change and resists change. The potential for influence of organizational members is not similar or symmetric, but rather the potential for change is distributed throughout the organization rather than concentrated at the top – which means that resistance travels inside the organization.

### The Role of Improvisation in Dissolving the Dualism

Addressing change and resistance to change from the minimalist perspective advanced by semi-structures and improvisation departs from the traditional assumption that change is planned and proceeds from the top-down. Semi-structures create space for improvisational activity. Improvisation, the process of making do with the available resources in the absence of planning, provides an event-driven, rather than an anticipation-driven approach to organizational change. While that which can be known in advance can be anticipated, the point about events is their inscrutability, their lack of predictability and rules (Deroy & Clegg, 2011). When events occur rules do not apply, by definition, and improvisation has to happen. Improvisation is imbued with paradoxical qualities and these are precisely what break frequent and traditional oppositions in organizational change/resistance. Dissolving the tensions opens new possibilities for appreciating the process of change and reframing the problem of resistance.

#### *Improvisation Is Planned* and *Unplanned*

A major issue in the opposition between change initiators and change recipients refers to their separation in organizational space and time: (a) initiators are at the top of the hierarchy, removed from implementing operations and mundane preoccupations and (b) moreover, they participate in the change process before other, 'lesser', organizational members. These layers of separation have the potential to create antagonisms rooted in the tension normally present in processes involving planning and execution. As Weick (2011, p. 13) puts it: 'Organizational change is resisted not just because the prospect of uncertainty is unsettling but because proposed changes seem too far removed from first-hand experience to have any relevance or meaning'. Duguid (2006, p. 1797) observes, 'workers may know more than managers about what is good for the company', an insight to which weight was recently added by Courpasson et al. (2012). Hence, improvised change or resistance from elsewhere in the organization than its 'strategic apex' may be wiser in import than that which is promulgated at a spatial and temporal distance. So-called 'high reliability organizations' (Weick & Sutcliffe, 2007) recognize that when the 'unexpected' happens, hierarchy may be suspended and the leading roles given to expert operators who improvise solutions ('with surprise comes the need to improvise'; p. 38) to contain damages and make the system resilient. Local improvisations may be a source of adaptation and a defence against unwanted surprises via alertness and responsiveness (Cunha, Clegg, & Kamoche, 2006). By freeing space for improvisation, rather than diminish accountability organizations create it at several organizational levels and turn improvisers into designer–practitioners of change.

The contribution of improvisation for reframing resistance consists in dissolving the boundaries between planning and execution. According to definitions, improvisation consists precisely in the convergence between planning and execution (Moorman & Miner, 1998): planners execute and executants plan as they go along. Temporal convergence opens the black box of change and presents change initiatives as conversations between those who define a direction and those that need to find the way to make it happen. The presentation of change as an improvisational journey reserves agentic spaces for change participants. Change, in other words, may sometimes be planned but that does not protect it against the normalcy of mess and *un*-design (Thomas & Hardy, 2011).

Planned and unplanned changes may be equally legitimate if improvisations do not breach the limits of legitimacy (Eisenhardt & Sull, 2001); of course, it is only through breaching behaviours that these limits become visible (Garfinkel, 1967). Improvisational actions, in this context, propagate ideas that can legitimately flow up the hierarchy to the extent that they are executively labelled desirable. By contrast, those ideas deemed illegitimate just circulate, seeding mutterings rather than management as formally designed. Such mutterings may, on occasion, seethe into discontent at the boundaries of legitimacy being drawn. The initiators and the recipients of improvised changes do not correspond to the 'usual suspects'. In fact, it takes unconventional management to accept that order may come from below rather than from the top and that hierarchy is not the only way of getting things done and defining the limits of legitimacy (Cunha, Rego, & Clegg, 2011).

### *Improvisation Is Controlled* and *Spontaneous*

Tightly controlled change seen only as a prerogative of managers generates resistance from those excluded from consideration – especially where it has significant implications for them. A series of negative effects are likely under such circumstances: members that would otherwise act as change initiators, showing initiative and proactivity, become demoralized; people at the top do not have the chance to recognize the worth of recommendations from the base and elsewhere; the deeply ingrained separation between thinkers and doers as a division of labour is heightened; and what people in operations see as the practical problems of the organization are not necessarily concerned with what strategic managers think, strategize and formulate – in part because the time spans of discretion can often be out of sync with each other (a point to be further developed below).

Improvisation offers a paradoxical space for both control and spontaneity. Instead of controlling via institutionalized micro-management, produced and reproduced by constraining bureaucracies, semi-structures blend control with freedom. They are the kind of enabling structures that control without stifling initiative (Kamoche & Cunha, 2001). In this sense there is guided spontaneity but this spontaneity occurs inside boundaries. Control is necessary for innovation to flourish but certain forms of control may actually hinder basic innovation – in a literal sense. The paradox of improvisation conceived as controlled and spontaneous action dissolves the tension between directed initiative, packaged at the top, and resistance as spontaneous challenge to the top's directives.

*Improvisation Is Abstract* and *Concrete*

A major cause of resistance to change lies in its abstract nature: recipients are expected to implement initiatives that they often do not understand. As Weick (2011) explains, change managers must work to 'reconcile macro designs with everyday problems that were not anticipated' (p. 17). Macro designs are inevitably too abstract to anticipate everyday (micro) developments, hence, micro–macro tensions and difficulties in bridging between the top and the base.

A strength of improvisation as a force for change consists in its simultaneously abstract and concrete nature. Improvisation is abstract because it relies on an infrastructure of simple rules (Davis, Eisenhardt, & Bingham, 2009) that need initial elaboration at a highly conceptual level but it is also concrete because it invites recipients to *translate* broad guidelines into local action (Sahlin & Wedlin, 2008). Semi-structures are delicate constructions that need constant revision to be sustained. It is easier to create structures that control too much or too little. Structures that control too much rely on the abstractness of rules on top of rules that govern behaviour from the bureau (as in *bureau*cracy). Structures that control too little may allow too much space for disconnected initiatives. The result appears as organizational drift (Ciborra, 2002). Here, organizations jump from opportunity to opportunity without a clear reason, spending time and wasting resources in non-synergistic ways and consuming executive attention in many complex landscapes without allowing the company to master any.

Seeing change as an improvisational process means that the organization will constantly balance conceptual configuration towards organizational coherence, while feeding and updating this effort to cohere with information from the frontline. Alert organizations know that managers need to centralize structuring and to decentralize information and decision-making to where expertise is (Weick & Roberts, 1993). Organizations that value improvisation thus travel between the conceptual power of semi-structuring and the concrete power of local initiative. Organizations that conceptualize too much are vulnerable in markets that change incessantly; organizations that conceptualize too little expose themselves to mindless reactivity. Neither is good.

Improvisation, in summary, provides a way out of the dualisms that oppose change stakeholders inside organizations. Improvisation is an invitation to see tension as a source rather than an obstacle to change when a duality perspective is adopted (Farjoun, 2010). With this, we are not defending the idea that organizations should not initiate change programmes or that resistance can be eliminated from the management of change. That would be too naïve: managers are supposed to manage and need to display their role as initiators and change programmes offer a superb opportunity to vent and expose the tensions staking out opposing organizational stakeholders. Ignoring the power of improvisation to reframe resistance to change should not be discounted, however. Improvisation offers a unique space for continuously negotiating the offers and counter-offers involved in change initiatives. It dissolves the barriers between initiation and reception. It combines planning as anticipation with planning while going along. It transforms labels and roles and suspends hierarchical rigidity. Departing from the established is not viewed in improvisation as a challenge to authority. Departing from habit is sanctioned by the organization and not against it.

Improvisation, in summary, is a process where the established orders of organizing are challenged and alternative orders are open to discovery. Interestingly, however, the subversive element of improvisation is not necessarily against management per se (Clegg, Kornberger, Carter, & Rhodes, 2006). It is a potential force that contains a measure of unpredictability but it is not premised on implacable hostility nor is it a panacea: its emergent traits may be threatening because when one starts improvising one does not know where improvisation will take one (see, e.g. Baker, Miner, & Eesley, 2003). Of course the same is valid for any other change process but in teleological models it does not have to be explicitly assumed). Ignoring emergence, however, is not the same as excluding it. As pointed out by Tsoukas and Dooley (2011, p. 731), 'improvisation is not an optional extra but permeates rule-governed behaviour.'

**Conclusion**

A reconsideration of resistance to change is underway in the organization and management literatures: promising to take us beyond simplistic dichotomizations towards embracing the complexity and realpolitik of change processes (Van de Ven & Sun, 2011). As is evident from the opening vignette concerning the Deepwater Horizon tragedy, a more sophisticated understanding of resistance to change has major implications for practice. However, assigning blame to contractors for deviance from systematic procedures is not as appropriate as working discursively with contractors in sustained relations and alliances (Pitsis, Clegg, Marosszeky, & Rura-Polley, 2003) in which change is sustained as an innovative practice rather than proscribed because of top-down systems.

Resistance has been viewed here as co-constitutive and embedded in power circuits, not as a more or less mechanistic action-reaction type of relationship. Resistance may initially be a concept derived from physics but it needs to be translated in its adoption into different scientific contexts: 'physics envy' (Flyvbjerg, 2002) should not inspire unreflective adoption.

Some authors advance different ways of understanding and leading change. Ford et al. (2008) invite managers to adopt discursive practices that alter the dynamics of change such as extensive communication, stimulating participation and building strong relationships. We went beyond this agent-centric perspective of change, however, and moved in the complementary direction of change as distributed process, suggesting that structural interventions may also help to diffuse resistance to change. Previous research has indicated that some simple interventions might produce relevant effects in organizational processes (Okhuysen & Eisenhardt, 2002). To this we would add that some interventions in the direction of simplicity, such as semi-structured improvisations, also stimulate adaptive complexity beyond established dualities.

Specifically, the role of minimalist semi-structures has been explored as a design in which improvisation may be cultivated and appreciated as forms of action that subverts and challenges traditional labels and roles of change management. The argument is consistent with recent defences of strategizing conceived as distributed strategy-making (Jarzabkowki, Balogun, & Seidl, 2007) and with the attribution of new roles to organizational members as initiators of change, namely those described as '*passionate drivers* – people who question the traditional way of doing things, dig into complex problems and stick with them until they are solved' (Hassan, 2011, p. 108). In improvisation, initiators and recipients shift roles, exchange offers and counter-offers between the top and the base, maintain designs that are incomplete by choice, engage in paradoxical relationships that subvert established labels and roles and allow change to keep its surprising component, understood as the source of the vitality of change as an organizing and disorganizing force. In this perspective, planned change is more focused on the gerund planning rather than the gerund changing.

In summary, we explored some possibilities opened by improvisation for the reconsideration of resistance to change. Change management focuses on the use of discourse and meaning as levers of organizational adaptation. The need for change, however, is not restricted to managers and employees: organizational scholars also have their responsibilities and need to regularly update their working ideas in response to changes in organizational landscapes. We contributed to this debate by exploring improvised change as a space for subverting and changing traditional categories of change management. Change managers have nothing to lose but the metaphorical chains tying them to conceptions of physics whose legitimacy does not translate from electric circuits of power to organizational circuits of power.

## Acknowledgement

This paper is part of a larger research project (CMU-PT/OUT/0014/2009).

## Funding

Miguel Pina e Cunha gratefully acknowledges support from Nova Forum. Support from the Portuguese Foundation for Science and Technology is gratefully acknowledged.

## Note

1. It is interesting to contrast this strategy of off-loading blame on to contractors with the assurances provided on its web pages concerned with sustainability and working with contractors: see http://www.bp.com/sectiongenericarticle800.do?categoryId=9040113&contentId=7073267, accessed March 10, 2013.

## References

Baker, T., Miner, A. S., & Eesley, D. T. (2003). Improvising firms: Bricolage, account giving and improvisational competencies in the founding process. *Research Policy*, *32*, 255–276.

Beer, M., Eisenstat, R. A., & Spector, B. (1990). Why change programs don't produce change. *Harvard Business Review*, *68*(6), 58–166.

Bingham, C., & Eisenhardt, K. M. (2011). Rational heuristics: The 'simple rules' that strategists learn from process experience. *Strategic Management Journal*, *32*, 1437–1464.

Brown, S. L., & Eisenhardt, K. M. (1997). The art of continuous change: Linking complexity theory and time-paced evolution in relentlessly shifting organizations. *Administrative Science Quarterly*, *42*, 1–34.

Ciborra, C. U. (2002). *The labyrinths of information*. Oxford: Oxford University Press.

Clegg, S. R. (1989). *Frameworks of power*. London: Sage.

Clegg, S. R., & Dunkerley, D. (1980). *Organization, class and control*. London: Routledge.

Clegg, S. R., Kornberger, M., Carter, C., & Rhodes, C. (2006). For management? *Management Learning*, *37*, 7–27.

Coch, L., & French, J. (1948). Overcoming resistance to change. *Human Relations*, *1*, 512–532.

Courpasson, D., Dany, F., & Clegg, S. (2012). Resisters at work: Generating productive resistance in the workplace. *Organization Science*, *23*(3), 801–819.

Cunha, M. P., Clegg, S. R., & Kamoche, K. (2006). Surprises in management and organization: Concept, sources, and a typology. *British Journal of Management*, *17*, 317–329.

Cunha, M. P., Rego, A., & Clegg, S. (2011). Beyond addiction: Hierarchy and other ways of getting things done. *European Management Journal*, *29*, 491–503.

Danisman, A. (2010). Good intentions and failed implementations: Understanding culture-based resistance to organizational change. *European Journal of Work and Organizational Psychology*, *19*(2), 200–220.

Davis, J. P., Eisenhardt, K. M., & Bingham, C. B. (2009). Optimal structure, market dynamism, and the strategy of simple rules. *Administrative Science Quarterly*, *54*, 413–452.

Deetz, S. (2008). Resistance: Would struggle by any other name be as sweet? *Management Communication Quarterly*, *21*(3), 387–392.

Dent, E. B., & Goldberg, S. G. (1999). Challenging 'resistance to change'. *Journal of Applied Behavioral Science*, *35*, 25–41.

Deroy, X., & Clegg, S. (2011). When events interact with business ethics. *Organization*, *18*, 637–653.

Dobosz-Bourne, D., & Jankowicz, A. D. (2006). Reframing resistance to change: Experience from General Motors Poland. *International Journal of Human Resource Management*, *17*, 2021–2034.

Duguid, P. (2006). What talking about machines tells us. *Organization Studies*, *27*, 1794–1804.

Eisenhardt, K. M., Furr, N. R., & Bingham, C. (2010). Microfoundations of performance: Balancing efficiency and flexibility in dynamic environments. *Organization Science*, *21*, 1263–1273.

Eisenhardt, K. M., & Sull, D. N. (2001). Strategy as simple rules. *Harvard Business Review*, *79*(1), 107–116.

Farjoun, M. (2010). Beyond dualism: Stability and change as a duality. *Academy of Management Review*, *35*(2), 202–225.

Fleming, P. (2008). Resistance to change. In S. Clegg & J. Bailey (Eds.), *International encyclopedia of organization studies* (Vol. 4, pp. 1376–1379). London: Sage.

Fleming, P., & Sewell, G. (2002). Looking for the good soldier, Svejk: Alternative modalities of resistance in the contemporary workplace. *Sociology*, *36*, 857–873.

Flyvbjerg, B. (2002). *Making social science matter; why social inquiry fails and how it can succeed again*. Cambridge: Cambridge University Press.

Ford, J. D., & Ford, L. W. (2009). Decoding resistance to change. *Harvard Business Review*, *87*(4), 99–103.

Ford, J. D., Ford, L. W., & D'Amelio, A. (2008). Resistance to change: The rest of the story. *Academy of Management Review*, *33*, 362–377.

Garfinkel, H. (1967). *Studies in ethnomethodology*. Englewood-Cliffs, NJ: Prentice-Hall.

Garud, R., Jain, S., & Tuertscher, P. (2008). Incomplete by design and designing for incompleteness. *Organization Studies*, *29*, 351–371.

Giangreco, A., & Peccei, R. (2005). The nature and antecedents of middle manager resistance to change: Evidence from an Italian context. *International Journal of Human Resource Management*, *16*, 1812–1829.

Graham, P. (1995). *Mary Parker Follett, prophet of management: A celebration of writings from the 1920s*. Boston, MA: Harvard Business School Press.

Hassan, F. (2011). The frontline advantage. *Harvard Business Review*, *89*(5), 106–114.

Jarzabkowki, P., Balogun, J., & Seidl, D. (2007). Strategizing: The challenges of a practice perspective. *Human Relations*, *60*, 5–27.

Kahn, W. A. (2011). Treating organizational wounds. *Organizational Dynamics*, *40*, 75–84.

Kamoche, K., & Cunha, M. P. (2001). Minimal structures: From jazz improvisation to product innovation. *Organization Studies*, *22*, 733–764.

Kerber, K., & Buono, A. F. (2005). Rethinking organizational change: Reframing the challenge of change management. *Organization Development Journal*, *23*(3), 23–38.

Kim, W. C., & Mauborgne, R. (2005). *Blue ocean strategy*. Boston, MA: Harvard Business School Press.

Kotter, J. P. (1996). *Leading change*. Boston, MA: Harvard Business School Press.

Kurke, L. E., Weick, K. E., & Ravlin, E. (1989). Can information loss be reversed? Evidence from serial reconstruction. *Communication Research*, *16*, 3–24.

Lawrence, P. R. (1954). How to overcome resistance to change. *Harvard Business Review*, *32*(3), 49–57.

Lewin, K. (1947). Frontiers in group dynamics. *Human Relations*, *1*, 5–41.

March, J. G. (1991). Exploration and exploitation in organizational life. *Organization Science*, *2*, 71–87.

Marion, R., & Uhl-Bien, M. (2011). Implications of complexity science for the study of leadership. In P. Allen, S. Maguire, & B. McKelvey (Eds.), *The Sage handbook of complexity and management* (pp. 385–399). Los Angeles, CA: Sage.

Meindl, J. R., Ehrlich, S. B., & Dukerich, J. M. (1985). The romance of leadership. *Administrative Science Quarterly*, *30*, 78–102.

Miller, D. (1990). *The Icarus paradox: How exceptional companies bring about their own fall*. New York, NY: HarperCollins.

Miller, H. (2013, February 25). BP accused of greed, lax safety at US oil spill trial, *AFP*. Retrieved March 10, 2013, from http://www.google.com/hostednews/afp/article/ALeqM5icx3MhuguOqb0cl9GXK4LdqvgGWg?docId=CNG.a5d63fecac928e636e3aad2cbef9433b.301

Moorman, C., & Miner, A. S. (1998). The convergence between planning and execution: Improvisation in new product development. *Journal of Marketing*, *62*, 1–20.

Nasim, S., & Sushil. (2011). Revisiting organizational change: Exploring the paradox of managing continuity and change. *Journal of Change Management*, *11*, 185–206.

Nickerson, J. A., & Zenger, T. R. (2002). Being efficiently fickle. A dynamic theory of organizational choice. *Organization Science*, *13*, 370–386.

Ocasio, W. (2008). Organizational change. In S. Clegg & J. Bailey (Eds.), *International encyclopedia of organization studies* (Vol. 3, pp. 1020–1024). London: Sage.

Okhuysen, G. A., & Eisenhardt, K. M. (2002). Integrating knowledge in groups: How formal interventions enable flexibility. *Organization Science*, *13*, 370–386.

Oreg, S., Vakola, M., & Armenakis, A. (2011). Change recipients' reactions to organizational change: A 60-year review of quantitative studies. *Journal of Applied Behavioral Science*, *47*(4), 461–524. doi: 10.1177/0021886310396550

O'Reilly, C. A., Harreld, J. B., & Tushman, M. L. (2009). Organizational ambidexterity: IBM and emerging business opportunities. *California Management Review*, *51*(4), 75–99.

Piderit, S. K. (2000). Rethinking resistance and recognizing ambivalence: A multidimensional view of attitudes toward an organizational change. *Academy of Management Review*, *25*, 783–794.

Pitsis, T., Clegg, S. R., Marosszeky, M., & Rura-Polley, T. (2003). Constructing the Olympic dream: Managing innovation through the future perfect. *Organization Science*, *14*(5), 574–590.

Plowman, D. A., Baker, L. T., Beck, T., Kulkarni, M., Solansky, S., & Travis, D. (2007). Radical change accidentally: The emergence and amplification of small change. *Academy of Management Journal*, *50*, 515–543.

Sahlin, K., & Wedlin, L. (2008). Circulating ideas: Imitation, translation and editing. In R. Greenwood, C. Oliver, K. Sahlin, & R. Suddaby (Eds.), *The Sage handbook of organizational institutionalism* (pp. 218–242). London: Sage.

Sorenson, J. B., & Stuart, T. (2000). Aging, obsolescence and organizational innovation. *Administrative Science Quarterly*, *45*, 81–112.

Stacey, R. (1991). *The chaos frontier*. London: Butterworth-Heinemann.

Thomas, R., & Hardy, C. (2011). Reframing resistance to change. *Scandinavian Journal of Management*, *27*(3), 322–331.

Tsoukas, H. (2005). Afterword: Why language matters in the analysis of organizational change. *Journal of Organizational Change Management*, *18*, 96–104.

Tsoukas, H., & Chia, R. (2002). On organizational becoming: Rethinking organizational change. *Organization Science*, *13*, 567–582.

Tsoukas, H., & Dooley, K. J. (2011). Introduction to the special issue: Towards the ecological style: Embracing complexity in organizational research. *Organization Studies*, *32*, 729–735.

Van de Ven, A. H., & Sun, K. (2011). Breakdowns in implementing models of organizational change. *Academy of Management Perspectives*, *25*(3), 58–74.

Ward, L. (2005, February 23). Managers still fight flexible working. *The Guardian*. Retrieved from http://www.guardian.co.uk/money/2005/feb/23/business.worklifebalance

Weick, K. E. (1979). *The social psychology of organizing* (2nd ed.). Reading, MA: Addison-Wesley.

Weick, K. E. (2011). Change agents as change poets – on reconnecting flux and hunches. *Journal of Change Management, 11*, 7–20.

Weick, K. E., & Roberts, K. (1993). Collective mind in organizations: Heedful interrelating on flight decks. *Administrative Science Quarterly, 38*, 357–381.

Weick, K. E., & Sutcliffe, K. M. (2007). *Managing the unexpected.* San Francisco, CA: Jossey-Bass.

# Advancing Sustainability Through Change and Innovation: A Co-evolutionary Perspective

SUZANNE BENN* & ELLEN BAKER**

*Australian Research Institute in Education for Sustainability, Macquarie University, Sydney, Australia,
**University of Technology, Sydney, Australia

ABSTRACT *This article addresses the problem of how change and innovation can create a fuller voice for ecological interests in organizations and public policy, raising issues about change mechanisms at the institutional versus organizational level. First, it suggests that the newer, systems-based and inclusive approaches to organizational development practice and theory may overcome shortcomings of earlier approaches to planned change. Second, it argues that co-evolutionary approaches that use complex adaptive systems thinking will more effectively structure such third-generation interventions by focusing on issues at the institutional level. Third, the article examines a dialectical model of institutional change which incorporates activist input and channels conflict into innovative outcomes. Finally, it presents a case example of how a dialectical model combined with a co-evolutionary perspective could foster the institutional change required to facilitate the integration of ecological priorities into the human systems of organizations.*

## Introduction

### *Ecological Sustainability and Innovation*

This article addresses the problem of how change and innovation can create a fuller voice for ecological interests in organizations and public policy through a critical evaluation of current approaches to organizational development and change.

The first section of the article points out shortcomings of earlier approaches to planned organizational development and change in relation to achieving ecological sustainability requirements. It is then suggested that the newer, systems-wide and inclusive approaches to organizational development practice and theory may overcome these limitations. As an example, the article explores co-evolutionary approaches that use complex adaptive systems thinking, arguing that such interventions will enable a focus on issues at the institutional level. A dialectical model of institutional change, which incorporates activist input and channels conflict into innovative outcomes, is then examined. The article then presents a case example of how a dialectical model combined with a co-evolutionary perspective, could foster the institutional change required to facilitate the integration of ecological priorities into organizational and public policy and decision-making.

A major challenge for organizations is how to balance and incorporate competing interests, values and constituencies (Quinn and Rohrbaugh, 1983; Buenger *et al.*, 1996). However, the now pressing debate on how to balance human requirements and economic priorities with ecological sustainability confronts managers with new and more difficult challenges. Non-human stakeholders are now to be considered as relevant stakeholders with whom it is important to build enduring and mutually beneficial relationships (Maak, 2007), with authoritative sources claiming impending conditions of crisis unless ecological issues are given more equal countenance in decision-making (Mooney *et al.*, 2005; Stern, 2006; Intergovernmental Panel on Climate Change, 2007). The urgency of the response lies in the need to address a major systems failure entailing a reassessment of the relationship between human and ecological systems (Coupland, 2005; Ehrenfeld, 2005).

At the level of the organization, the multiple strategies, modes of assessment and required standards of ecological sustainability, such as industrial ecology, eco-efficiency and strategic proactivity, point to a highly complex task if such innovations are to be implemented (McDonough and Braungart, 2002; Winn and Zietsma, 2004; Jamali, 2006; Kallio and Nordberg, 2006; Tregigda and Milne, 2006; Dunphy *et al.*, 2007; Waage, 2007). It is important to note that innovation within the context of sustainability may not be the same as innovation in other contexts. Hall and Vredenburg (2003), for example, report that managers have had great difficulty when trying to innovate under pressures from sustainable development. Managers find their innovation strategies are inadequate to accommodate the highly complex and uncertain nature of these new demands. Their previous strategies do not incorporate the constraints of the social and environmental pressures, which involve a wider range of stakeholders as well as more ambiguous and contradictory demands. Stakeholders may include environmental activists, safety advocates and local interests, with different priorities, often less focussed on technical aspects of innovation, as well as the more usual stakeholders such as customers, suppliers or investors (Hall and Martin, 2005).

This article assumes that organizations will need to make fundamental changes in the way they conduct business and work within the tenets of ‘stronger’ versions of sustainability, to ensure human needs do not diminish the supply of natural capital available for future generations (Turner, 1992; Daly, 1996). An accepted body of thought within the corporate sustainability literature is that such an outcome can only be achieved through high levels of innovation within the organization, leading to product, process or service redesign (Rodriguez *et al.*, 2002; Snyder and Duarte, 2003; Hart, 2005; Laszlo, 2008). However, this literature leaves unanswered the question of how to go beyond technical innovation to engender the paradigmatic change that incorporating ecological values entails.

The following section of the article critically evaluates the organizational development approach of planned change in light of this requirement. Some critical limitations of the earlier organizational development approaches are identified, particularly in relation to organizational complexity and the relationship between human and ecological systems. Some of the advances of more recent interpretations are noted in this regard.

## Innovation, Sustainability and Organizational Development

### *Earlier Approaches to Organizational Development*

Organization development is traditionally described as the process by which an organization can achieve its mission and build long-term success. It is defined here as a highly planned program of change and development using behavioral science knowledge, geared towards a particular organizational outcome (Beckhard, 1969; Cummins and Worley, 2004; Seo *et al.*, 2004). The claimed systemic impacts of earlier approaches to planned change such as action research and team building are undermined by their individual or group level focus (Seo *et al.*, 2004). For the purpose of addressing change that might give a fuller voice to ecological interests, such an approach is particularly inappropriate given the holistic, systems-wide intervention required to establish a more dynamic relationship between the ecological and human systems of the organization (Milne *et al.*, 2006). It does not have the capacity to drive the fundamental innovations and radical change required to implement ecological values such as intergenerational equity and interconnectedness (Driscoll and Starik, 2004) and address the now pressing environmental concerns such as climate change associated with business activity (Bartunek *et al.*, 2006; Maguire and Hardy, 2009).

The earlier versions of the planned approach to change are constrained in their capacity to deal with the complexity of interrelationships between the natural environment, organizations and their employees (Dobers and Wolf, 1999; Law, 2004; Sandstrom, 2007). Both the first generation (action research, sensitivity training) and second generation (transformational change, future search) iterations (Seo *et al.*, 2004) of planned change tend to interpret nature/employee, employee/organization, and organization/nature as dualistic entities. Implementing change according to a pre-determined goal and through the lens of such polarities has problems, given the 'complex reality' of assessing ecological performance (Kolk and Mauser, 2002, p. 25) and the many contingency factors that need to be considered in its specification (Jermier *et al.*, 2006). At a practical level, these include the type of program (pollution prevention, waste management, and sustainable management systems), as well as sectoral characteristics (Orsato, 2004; Ramus and Montiel, 2005) and the increasing differences in ecological performance between organizations (York, 2004).

### *Contemporary Organizational Development Approaches*

Recent work in what Seo *et al.* (2004) term third-generation organizational development has the capacity to address these limitations. Third-generation organizational development approaches, such as learning organization and appreciative inquiry, and including process interventions such as open-space technology aim at transformational change. Yet in contrast to second-generation organizational development, they work on the premise that the past does not have to be totally rejected for radical change to occur. These approaches are not static and they allow for systems-wide interventions, the incorporation of visioning or futuring and representation of a wide range of stakeholder viewpoints (Waddell *et al.*, 2007). In line with these approaches, some action research has also shifted to a whole systems approach to incorporate a wider range of stakeholders. So, for example, leading action research specialists now focus on inquiry that contributes to the wellbeing of human communities and the ecosystems within which they co-exist (Reason, 2006). A recent definition of action research defines its wide purpose as:

> to contribute to the increased well-being – economic, political, psychological, spiritual – of humanity, and to a more equitable and sustainable relationship with the wider ecology of the planet of which we are an intrinsic part (Reason and Bradbury, 2001, p. 2).

Other contemporary exponents of organizational development working within this third-generation approach contend that there is a need to move from what Anderson and Anderson (2001) have termed the Industrial Mindset, reflecting the dynamics of closed systems, to the Emerging Mindset where reality is portrayed as a living system, all components are perceived as interconnected and interdependent, and life is seen as continuous, rather than composed of discrete elements. It is argued that systems-wide process interventions can bring about a shift from the Industrial Mindset and transform leader and employee behavior within the organization. However, the question raised in this article is how to bring about change from the Industrial Mindset at an institutional level. How can third-generation organizational development approaches be focussed at the level of institutional change? What are the processes, for instance, that allow for deinstitutionalisation (Dacin *et al.*, 2002) and the disappearance of the beliefs, ideas and practices associated with the Industrial Mindset?

## Towards Institutional-level Change and Innovation

### *The Organization as Complex Adaptive System*

In the following sections of this article, it is argued that co-evolutionary approaches that use complex adaptive systems (CAS) thinking and incorporate dialectical collective action processes can be useful to structure interventions so that they focus change at the institutional level. Using a case example of a long-running environmental dispute, the article then discusses how such an approach can be enabled and embedded.

The article begins with a discussion of why viewing an organization as a CAS is useful concerning its aim to explore how to give fuller voice to ecological values. Overall, the complexity of today's organizations increases the need to conceptualize the relationship between human and ecological systems within a more dynamic framework. In an article on 'post- bureaucracy', Clegg (forthcoming) argues that bureaucracy, far from being superseded, is becoming embroiled in complex processes of hybridization and that bureaucracies are simultaneously decomposing and recomposing. In the latter, the bureaucrat is being replaced by the project leader. Such depictions of organizational life fit well with viewing the organization as a CAS and suggest reconceptualizing the relationship between the human and ecological systems of the organization within that context.

CAS are neural-like networks of interacting, interdependent agents who are bonded by common goals, outlooks and needs. They are changeable structures with multiple overlapping hierarchies, and like the individuals that comprise them, CAS are linked to one another in an interactive network (Uhl-Bien *et al.*, 2007, p. 299). The metaphor of CAS has been widely put to use in the organizational studies and management literatures to highlight organizational and inter-organizational properties such as the dynamic interaction between organizations and associated systemic evolution through recombination (Cornelissen and Kafouros, 2008).

### *Co-evolutionary Approaches to Innovation and change*

Within the CAS context, organizational adaptations co-evolve with changes in the external environment. The metaphor of organizational co-evolution is drawn from the biological concept of co-evolution – that two species or populations may evolve, each adapting to the other. The next section explores the applicability of co-evolution in CAS in the context of sustainability.

Viewing organizational sustainability through the lens of the CAS metaphor has been supported by an ever-increasing number of authors (for examples, Berkes *et al.*, 2003; Pahl-Wostl, 2007; Rammel *et al.*, 2007), concomitant with the identified need to apply frameworks, approaches and philosophies that take a holistic approach (Ramos-Martin, 2003). Similarly, a CAS perspective is seen across organizational and environmental literature (Kallio and Nordberg, 2006), with a common entreaty to move beyond fragmented, mechanistic views of ecological problems and solutions (Clark, 1994; Hoffman, 2006). A linear view on change is recognized in this literature as unsuitable and inadequate for modelling systems with interconnections and feedback loops (Anderson, 1999; Glor, 2007).

Rather than a linear relationship between the planned development of the human systems of the organization and ecological sustainability, a more dynamic understanding would thus predict that 'change may occur rapidly or slowly; it may accumulate linearly or nonlinearly, it may be constant or have bursts of punctuated equilibrium' (Dooley, 1997, p. 89). Even the assumption that the individual elements of the human and ecological systems can be identified in order to establish a causal relationship needs to be rethought when viewed through the CAS lens. Complex systems cannot be reduced to basic elements and so cannot be recombined in lawful ways to explain characteristics; thus such systems need to be studied as whole entities/systems or patterns of behavior (Glor, 2007)

A further consideration that can be drawn from the CAS metaphor is the inherent interconnection between organizations and the larger systems within which they are located. As discussed above, this has implications for the way it is conceptualized that innovations develop in organizations, but it also can inform about how organizations must change to adapt to their wider environment – in the terms used in this article, the ecosystem.

Sustainability draws on the interrelatedness of technological, social, political, and ecological systems and sub-systems. The following section argues that the relationship between human and ecological systems should be reconceptualized in terms of a dynamic co-evolution towards sustainability. Such an approach, based in conditions of mutual influence, it is argued, could result in the transformational changes at the institutional level that are required if organizations and public policy formation are to reframe around incorporating ecological concerns. As Maguire and Hardy (2009) argue, institutional change and particularly, deinstitutionalisation, is highly relevant in a world where long-accepted business practices may have negative effects on society and on the natural environment.

This problem is broadly addressed in the natural resource management (NRM) literature, where leading scholars argue that the complexity of ecosystem needs means a 'need for smaller-scale, more environmentally sound and more democratic and nested natural resource management systems that are self-organizing, adaptive and resilient' (Berkes *et al.*, 2003, p. 21). Such an approach recognizes that humans are part of the system and, therefore, part of the problem and that mutual adaptation may be the answer.

This context of a co-evolutionary perspective on organizations can also learn from evolutionary and ecological economists. Arguably, Norgaard's (1994) theory on co-evolution is a highly relevant approach that could be taken up as a framework for progressing sustainability at an organizational level. On this view:

> Development is a process of co-evolution between knowledge, values, organization, technology and the environment. Each of these sub-systems is related to each of the others, yet each is also changing and effecting change in the others......and with each sub-system putting selective pressure on each of the others they co-evolve in a manner where each reflects the other. (Norgaard, 1994, p. 216)

So, for example, social norms, practices and attitudes need to evolve so that they incorporate ecological concerns, as well as the reverse. In an approach drawing on ecological economics, Rammel *et al.*'s (2007) analysis of CAS leads to their recommendation that institutions (and organizations) need to take a co-evolutionary perspective to progress sustainability. On this argument, organizational learning systems need to be developed to obtain higher levels of recognition of the socio-economic adaptations that emerge within institutions, their impact on the natural environment, and vice versa. An example of this co-evolutionary approach is the way that norms and practices of community-based management systems have co-evolved with their resource base. As Dove (1993) points out in his study of forestry use in Pakistan, the efficacy of applying this approach is dependent upon feedback from the ecosystem to the sociosystem, in turn dependent upon the accurate perceptions of the process by the participating population.

To explicitly take this view of human-ecological sustainability as co-evolutionary, it is necessary to understand that beyond the intertwined nature of human and ecological systems is the fact that human systems, as opposed to ecological systems, are self-reflexive and self-aware (Kay and Regier, 2000), lending strength to the notion that innovations, if enabled within a co-evolutionary framework, could develop more in line with ecological sustainability – given that humans are by their very nature a part of the ecology. However, as Porter (2006) points out, careful consideration needs to be given to the co-relationship between human and ecological systems, since one entity is meaning making, involving the conscious and therefore rapid sharing of knowledge, while the other is not.

These considerations of the organization within a co-evolutionary perspective support the claim made in this article for innovation and change at the institutional level – reaching beyond the boundaries of the individual organization to deliver an established, radically changed pattern of norms and practices that recognize the interconnection between the elements of sustainability in the context of business and public policy formation. Yet it raises the key question – how to prompt the functional interdependence of social and ecological systems so that they 'change together via constant change in both systems' (Arrow *et al.*, 2000, p. 207).

## Generating Institutional Innovation

### *Dialectical Processes and Mutual Influence*

Hargrave and Van de Ven (2006) offer an important view on innovation at the institutional level that is highly relevant to the challenge of implementing a radical and paradigmatic shift through co-evolutionary approaches to sustainability. Drawing from social movement and innovation management literature, these authors see institutional change as a dialectical process where the ongoing contestation between competing actors results in the synthesis of new institutions.

In their model of collective change, networks of activists representing partisan viewpoints engage in a collective process that can create or revise institutions. Clearly, the dialectical process involves issues of power, as well as conflict. The suggestion is that this collective action model of innovation is most appropriate at the '*developmental phase* of institutional change, when networks of actors emerge to introduce competing alternative approaches or designs that entail different proposals for institutional change' (Hargrave and Van de Ven, 2006, p. 883). Actors contribute to the creative process when they have sufficient resources to do so. This model offers suggestions on how the co-evolutionary relationship based on patterns of mutual influence between the social and ecological sustainability elements could be established.

Such a perspective on innovation has particularly radical implications for the influence that could be exerted from the ecological system. The time is ripe for these 'partisan actors' to include environmental activists. Now resources are available to be harnessed in this collective process in order to represent the ecological system as a stakeholder (Starik, 1995). Such available resources include concerned employees at various levels, environmental NGOs and activists, as well as international organizations such as the Inter-Governmental Panel on Climate Change.

It should be noted that it is the dialectical interaction between the actors that generates innovation and change. The following case provides an example of a societal dilemma where such interactions between multiple actors have prompted innovations that reflect some progress towards the introduction of ecological values and norms into organizational thinking and public policy making.

### *The Case of Decision-making on HCB*

The case of decision-making concerning the largest store in the world of the so-called intractable waste, hexachlorobenzene (HCB), stockpiled in the grounds of the Orica chemicals company on the shores of Botany Bay, Sydney, is well described elsewhere (Benn and Jones, 2009; Brown, 2009). For the purposes of the argument presented in this article, however, the case highlights how Hargrave and Van de Ven's (2006) model may play out with resulting shifts in accepted ideas, norms and practices in decision-making concerning toxic waste and how dialectical processes can generate a co-evolutionary model of change.

The story of this HCB waste begins during World War II, when it was produced as a by-product of the industrial processes conducted by ICI Australia, on the site that is now Orica, at Botany Bay. Although these processes were halted in the 1970s, 10,000 tonnes of this carcinogenic compound, now classified under the Stockholm Convention as a persistent organic pollutant, remain stored in specially prepared drums on the site, awaiting a decision as to their disposal.

A 1992 decision by the Australian Government, rejecting the construction of a High Temperature Incinerator (HTI) at various rural sites in Australia due to community opposition, prompted a study of other available technologies and sowed the seeds for possible decision-making allowing disposal of the waste on site in the once industrial but now increasingly suburban area of Botany. However, also prompted by increased community recognition of the risks associated with toxic chemicals, in 1992 the Government established a Community Participation and Review Committee (CPRC) constituting Orica, other local business and industry interests, local community representatives, local and national environmental organizations, state and national government representatives and local government (Rae and Brown, 2009). The CPRC was charged with the responsibility of reviewing information concerning the disposal of the waste and of advising the government and Orica in this regard.

The diverse composition of the CPRC and the active facilitation at its regular meetings by a skilled and independent Chair has ensured robust debate, openly conducted within this forum. All interests represented on the CPRC have shown remarkable tenacity in pursuing its mission, ongoing now for 17 years. Local environmental activists within the CPRC have been strongly supported by the wider environmental organizations and environmental justice networks in Australia, with the focus being on the building capacity of the local community so that they could engage more effectively with the highly scientific issues underpinning the decision-making concerning disposal of the waste (Lloyd-Smith, 2009). Local government, too, has given support to the ongoing functioning of the CPRC as a forum for interaction between the stakeholders (Hillier *et al.*, 2009).

While, as yet no decision has been made on how to destroy the waste,[1] the CPRC has been a vehicle for institutional change engendered by the dialectical interchange between these various actors. The interchange, often but not always, involving major disputations (Brown, 2009; Jensen-Lee, 2009) has pushed new understandings of the need for community consultation at Orica, with radically different corporate protocols now in place to convey and receive information concerning its environmental impacts on the local community (Brown, 2009). The rejection by an Independent Panel of Orica's claims to the right to destroy the waste on site reflects changes to the previously accepted practice in Australia that companies can generate toxic waste through often polluting industrial processes and then externalize their social and environmental costs – expecting the local human and ecological communities to 'carry the burden of their remediation' (Grace, 2009). Such practices had been institutionalized through the supervisory activities of governments long accustomed to co-locate polluting industry and working-class populations in areas such as Botany (James, 2009). The fact that there has been no decision made as yet on how to destroy the waste does not, therefore, diminish our point that the CPRC forum, by enabling the interaction and debate between the multiple actors engaged with this dilemma, has prompted innovations concerning the implementation of ecological values into corporate and government decision-making.

Crucially, it has altered a view of what constitutes legitimate knowledge concerning environmental risk associated with toxic chemicals. As citizens' concerns regarding the quality and long-term impacts of waste disposal techniques gained legitimacy (partly through their determination to develop their own knowledge around complex issues of toxic risk), their understanding of normative practice has become incorporated into the various Commissions of Inquiry and other institutional effects associated with toxic waste in Australia (Healy, 2009). Key to this transfer in legitimacy has been an identity shift for Orica. The dispute concerning disposal has seen the influence of a high-profile science and technology-based organization about how the waste should be destroyed now challenged by the growing symbolic capital of the CPRC as an entity, a factor strongly linked to the preparedness of the members to engage in informed and ongoing dialogue within its forum (Benn and Jones, 2009; Hillier *et al.*, 2009). In particular, legitimacy is increasingly accorded to the voices of local environmental activists – with their leader, now aged over 80 years, recently accorded Australia's major public honour, the Order of Australia.

From the argument presented in this article, this case example demonstrates the widening and diverse constellation of stakeholders prepared to represent the ecological system, now energised and committed to such an extent that it can engage in collaborative networking with actors representing other ecological elements. These interactions, along with the often confrontational debates engaged in over the years through the CPRC forum, have pushed government and corporate policymaking in Australia to address the right for ecological and community interests to be recognized in decisions such as the disposal of toxic waste. The effect has been to establish a pattern of co-evolution between the social and ecological systems implicated in this issue. The case provides an example of how the mutual adaptation between social and ecological systems can be enabled, as new social norms, decision-making structures and processes of community engagement evolve in dynamic interaction with emergent ecological values (see Figure 1).

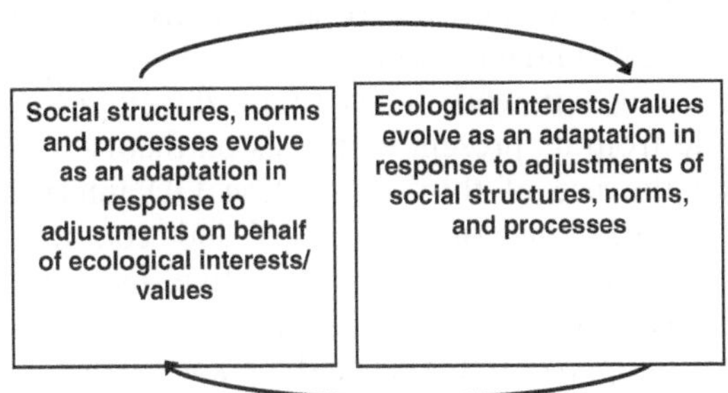


**Figure 1.** Co-evolution of social and ecological interests.

As empowered local activists have adapted by developing high levels of scientific knowledge around issues of toxic risk, enabling them to engage in an ongoing argumentation concerning the environmental risks associated with disposal of the waste on site, they have forced adaptation in the social system, reflected in new norms and practices concerning community consultation around environmental impacts of industrial processes. The case also supports Glynn and Abzug's (2002) findings concerning the relationship between identity shifts and the legitimacy accorded to actors, processes or structures that underpin such changes at the institutional level. The struggle has been about legitimacy, in this case of scientific versus lay knowledge.

In summary, the HCB case highlights a number of key points in the argument concerning the conditions underpinning institutional change on behalf of ecological values. Firstly, it shows how a systems-based approach, incorporating capacity building to enable effective dialectical interaction between all concerned stakeholders, can enable institutional change. This approach can be supported through what we have termed (following Seo *et al.*, 2004) third-generation organizational development. In that sense, the human systems can be developed so that they can co-evolve with the ecological systems.

Relating this case to Hargrave and Van de Ven's thesis about institutional-level change (2006), it is suggested that groups of 'ecological' activists will emerge who are distanced enough from current institutionalised perspectives on the way business should be conducted, that they will engage in dialectic interaction out of which paradigmatic change can occur. It is further suggested that the importance of appropriately facilitated system-wide fora as sites for such interaction and in the context of which actors representing ecological interests can be supported so that they have equal voice with other interests.

An alternative approach to explaining institutional-level change is to view it as the harnessing of collective action to displace entrenched interests (Rao, 2009). Rao employs the concepts of 'market rebels' (activists that defy authority and convention), 'hot causes' (constructions that arouse intense emotions) and 'cool mobilization' (unconventional techniques that engage audiences in collective action). He also emphasises the importance of thinking like an activist, forging a collective identity and mobilizing support when trying to initiate social innovation. Rao's approach, although coming from a social-movement literature base, has much in common with the thesis of this article. Rao presents case studies from many different contexts to support his argument and these case studies provide practical guidance which is complementary to this article and could be integrated with our work in its future development. For example, in extending this article from its present emphasis on theory into relevant practice, one could integrate the use of third generation OD interventions with Rao's advice to activists (based on use of 'hot causes' and 'cool mobilization') to help organizational employees to start thinking more like insurgents. This integration would assist in overcoming a current limitation in this article, the large gap between the theoretical approach it takes and the knowledge that will be required to put it into practice.

## Conclusion

The process of co-evolution, or the process of alignment between different entities in CAS, involves unplanned innovations, emergent and operating at the edge of chaos. Crucial to ensuring the counterforce required on behalf of ecological systems, so they can participate in the dialectical struggle discussed above, is the creation and facilitation of appropriate fora (Carson, 2009). It is here that the more recent advances in organizational development that involve dialectical representation from all stakeholders are relevant in generating interaction at an institutional level.

This article concludes with the point that utilizing third-generation organizational development approaches in the context of the organization as CAS can, facilitates the co-evolution that may enable ecological interests to be institutionalized while deinstitutionalizing those business and industrial practices antagonistic to such values. It is also suggested that the co-evolutionary decision- making systems and fora that are developed around ecological issues may generate useful systems, ideas, models and networks that could then serve to help both business and government — corporate and public policy-makers — generate change and innovation about issues that arise in organizational core functions that are outside the direct concerns of environmental sustainability.

## Note

1. Most recent attempts at a conclusion to the long-running dispute involve negotiations with Denmark in order to export the waste to be destroyed by HTI in that country. This follows a 2007 decision by the Australian Government to export it to Germany for HTI destruction and the subsequent ruling by German jurisdictions that the HCB import would be illegal (Brown, 2009)

## References

Anderson, D. and Anderson, L. (2001) *Beyond Change Management* (San Francisco: Jossey-Bass Pfeiffer).

Anderson, P. (1999) Complexity theory and organisation science, *Organisation Science*, 10, pp. 216–232.

Arrow, H., McGrath, J. and Berdahl, J. (2000) *Small Groups as Complex Systems*, 2nd edn (Thousand Oaks: Sage Publications).

Bartunek, J., Rynes, S. and Ireland, D. (2006) What makes management research interesting and why does it matter? *Academy of Management Journal*, 49, pp. 9–15.

Beckhard, R. (1969) *Organisation Development: Strategies and Models* (Reading, MA: Addison-Wesley).

Benn, S. and Jones, R. (2009) Forming corporate identity: symbolic capital, industry perspectives and community participation, in: P. Brown and S. Benn (eds) *Journal of Environmental Management*, 90(4), pp. 1593–1604.

Berkes, F., Colding, J. and Folke, C. (2003) Introduction, in: F. Berkes, J. Colding and C. Folke (eds) *Navigating Social-ecological Systems: Building Resilience for Complexity and Change*, pp. 1–30 (Cambridge: Cambridge University Press).

Brown, P. (2009) Toxic waste in our midst: the case of hexachlorbenzene, in: P. Brown and S. Benn (eds) *Journal of Environmental Management*, 90(4), pp. 1559–1567.

Buenger, V., Draft, R.L., Conlon, E.J. and Austin, J. (1996) Competing values in organisations: contextual influences and structural consequences, *Organisational Science*, 7(5), pp. 557–576.

Carson, L. (2009) Deliberative public participation and hexachlorbenzene stockpiles, in: P. Brown and S. Benn (eds), *Journal of Environmental Management*, 90(4), pp. 1636–1643.

Clark, M.E. (1994) Integrating human needs into our vision of sustainability, *Futures*, 26(2), pp. 180–184.

Clegg, S.R. (forthcoming) Under reconstruction: modern bureaucracies, in: M. Harris, H. Höpfl and S.R. Clegg (eds) *Managing Modernity* (London: Routledge).

Cornelisson, J. and Kafouros, M. (2008) The emergent organisation: primary and complex metaphors in theorizing about organisations, *Organisation Studies*, 29, pp. 957–978.

Coupland, C. (2005) Corporate social responsibility as argument on the web, *Journal of Business Ethics*, 62, pp. 355–366.

Cummins, T. and Worley, C. (2004) *Organisation Development and Change*, 8th edn (Cincinnati, OH: South-Western Publishing).

Dacin, M., Goodstein, J. and Scott, W. (2002) Institutional theory and institutional change: introduction to the special issue forum, *Academy of Management Journal*, 45, pp. 45–57.

Daly, H. (1996) *Beyond Growth: The Economics of Sustainable Development* (Boston, MA: Beacon Press).

Dobers, P. and Wolff, R. (1999) Eco-efficiency and dematerialisation: scenarios for new industrial logics in recycling industries, automobile and household appliances, *Business Strategy and the Environment*, 8, pp. 31–45.

Dooley, K.J. (1997) A complex adaptive systems model of organization change, *Nonlinear Dynamics, Psychology, and Life Sciences*, 1, pp. 69–97.

Dove, M. (1993) The co-evolution of population and environment: the ecology and ideology of feedback relations in Pakistan, *Population and Environment*, 15, pp. 89–111.

Driscoll, C. and Starik, M. (2004) The primordial stakeholder: advancing the conceptual consideration of stakeholder status for the natural environment, *Journal of Business Ethics*, 49, pp. 55–73.

Dunphy, D., Griffiths, A. and Benn, S. (2007) *Organisational Change for Corporate Sustainability* (London and New York: Routledge).

Ehrenfeld, J. (2005) The roots of sustainability, *MIT Sloan Management Review*, 46, pp. 23–27.

Glor, E.D. (2007) Assessing organisational capacity to adapt, *Emergence: Complexity and Organisation*, 9, pp. 33–46.

Glynn, M. and Abzug, R. (2002) Institutionalising identity: symbolic isomorphism and organizational names, *Academy of Management Journal*, 45(1), pp. 267–280.

Grace, D. (2009) Errant corporations, diffuse responsibilities, and the environment: ethical issues in the Orica case study, in: P. Brown and S. Benn (eds) *Journal of Environmental Management*, 90(4), pp. 1622–1627.

Hall, J. and Martin, M. (2005) Disruptive technologies, stakeholders and the innovation value-added chain: a framework for evaluating radical technology development, *R&D Management*, 35(3), pp. 273–284.

Hall, J. and Vredenburg, H. (2003) The challenges of innovating for sustainable development, *MIT Sloan Management Review*, 45(1), pp. 61–68.

Hargrave, T. and Van de Ven, A. (2006) A collective action model of institutional innovation, *Academy of Management Review*, 31(4), pp. 864–888.

Hart, S.L. (2005) Innovation, creative destruction and sustainability, *Research Technology Management*, 48, pp. 21–27.

Healy, S. (2009) Towards an epistemology of public participation, in: P. Brown and S. Benn (eds) *Journal of Environmental Management*, 90(4), pp. 1644–1654.

Hillier, N., Genissen, J., Pickering, B. and Solesnki, R. (2009) With an introduction by Paul Brown, Our battle with hexachlorbenzene: citizen perspectives on toxic waste in Botany, in: P. Brown and S. Benn (eds) *Journal of Environmental Management*, 90(4), pp. 1605–1612.

Hoffman, A.J. (2006) Linking social systems analysis to the industrial ecology framework, *Organisation and Environment*, 19(4), pp. 439–457.

Intergovernmental Panel on Climate Change (2007) *Intergovernmental Panel on Climate Change Fourth Assessment Report*, Available at http://www.ipcc.ch/ (accessed 19 September 2009).

Jamali, D. (2006) Insights into triple bottom line integration from a learning organisation perspective, *Business Process Management Journal*, 12, pp. 809–821.

James, P. (2009) The supervision of environmental risk: the case of HCB waste or Botany/ Randwick? in: P. Brown and S. Benn (eds) *Journal of Environmental Management*, 90(4), pp. 1576–1582.

Jensen-Lee, C. (2009) When unequals are treated equally: the 2002 commission of inquiry into Orica's Geomelt proposal, in: P. Brown and S. Benn (eds) *Journal of Environmental Management*, 90(4), pp. 1613–1621.

Jermier, J., Forbes, L., Benn, S. and Orsato, R. (2006) The new corporate environmentalism and green politics, in: S. Clegg, C. Hardy, T. Lawrence and W. Nord (eds) *The Sage Handbook of Organisational Studies*, pp. 618–650 (London: Sage Publications).

Kallio, T. and Nordberg, P. (2006) The evolution of organisations and natural environment discourse, *Organisation & Environment*, 19, pp. 439–457.

Kay, J.J. and Regier, H. (2000) Uncertainty, complexity and ecological integrity: Insights from an ecosystem approach, in: P. Crabbe, A. Holland, L. Ryszkowski and L. Westra (eds) *Implementing Ecological Integrity: Restoring Regional and Global Environmental and Human Health*, NATO Science Series, Environmental Security, pp. 121–156 (Dordrecht: Kluwer).

Kolk, A. and Mauser, A. (2002) The evolution of environmental management: from stage models to performance evaluation, *Business Strategy and the Environment*, 11, pp. 114–131.

Laszlo, C. (2008) *Sustainable Value: How the World's Leading Companies are Doing Well by Doing Good* (Palo Alto, CA: Stanford University Press).

Law, J. (2004) *After Method: Mess in Social Science Research* (London: Routledge).

Lloyd-Smith, M. (2009) Information, power and environmental justice in Botany: the role of community information systems, in: P. Brown and S. Benn (eds) *Journal of Environmental Management*, 90(4), pp. 1628–1635.

Maak, T. (2007) Responsible leadership, stakeholder engagement, and the emergence of social capital, *Journal of Business Ethics*, 74(4), pp. 329–344.

Maguire, S. and Hardy, C. (2009) Discourse and deinstitutionalisation: the decline of DDT, *Academy of Management Journal*, 52(1), pp. 148–178.

McDonough, W. and Braungart, M. (2002) Design for the triple top line: new tools for sustainable commerce, *Corporate Environmental Strategy*, 9, pp. 251–258.

Milne, M., Kearins, K. and Walton, S. (2006) Business makes a 'journey' out of 'sustainability': creating adventures in Wonderland? *Organisation*, 13(6), pp. 801–839.

Mooney, H., Cropper, A. and Reid, W. (2005) Confronting the human dilemma, *Nature*, 434, pp. 561–562.

Norgaard, R. (1994) The co-evolution of economic and environmental systems and the emergence of unsustainability, in: R. England (ed) *Evolutionary Concepts in Contemporary Economics*, pp. 213–224 (Michigan: University of Michigan Press).

Orsato, R.J. (2004) The ecological modernization of organizational fields, in: S. Sharma and M. Starik (eds) *New Perspectives in Research on Corporate Sustainability: Stakeholders, Environment and Society*, pp. 270–306 (London: Edward Elgar).

Pahl-Wostl, C. (2007) The implications of complexity for integrated resources management, *Environmental Modelling & Software*, 22, pp. 561–569.

Porter, T.B. (2006) Co-evolution as a research framework for organisations and the natural environment, *Organisation & Environment*, 19(4), pp. 479–506.

Quinn, R.E. and Rohrbaugh, J. (1983) A spatial model of effectiveness criteria: towards a competing values approach to organisational analysis, *Management Science*, 29, pp. 363–377.

Rae, I. and Brown, P. (2009) Managing the intractable: communicative structures for the management of hexachorobenzene and other scheduled wastes, in: P. Brown and S. Benn (eds) *Journal of Environmental Management*, 90(4), pp. 1583–1592.

Rammel, C., Stagl, S. and Wilfing, H. (2007) Managing complex adaptive systems – a co-evolutionary perspective on natural resource management, *Ecological Economics*, 63, pp. 9–21.

Ramos-Martin, J. (2003) Empiricism in ecological economics: a perspective from complex systems theory, *Ecological Economics*, 46, pp. 387–398.

Ramus, C. and Monteil, I. (2005) When are corporate environmental policies a form of greenwashing? *Business and Society*, 44, pp. 377–414.

Rao, H. (2009) *Market Rebels: How Activists Make or Break Radical Innovations* (Princeton: Princeton University Press).

Reason, P. (2006) Choice and quality in action research practice, *Journal of Management Inquiry*, 15(2), pp. 187–203.

Reason, P. and Bradbury, H. (2001) Inquiry and participation in search of a world worthy of human aspiration, in: P. Reason and H. Bradbury (eds) *Handbook of Action Research: Participative Inquiry and Practice*, pp. 1–14 (Los Angeles: Sage Publications).

Rodriguez, M., Ricart, J. and Sanchez, P. (2002) Sustainable development and the sustainability of competitive advantage, *Creativity and Innovation Management*, 11, pp. 135–146.

Sandstrom, J. (2007) Extending the discourse in research on corporate sustainability, *Innovation & Sustainable Development*, 1, pp. 153–167.

Seo, M., Putnam, L. and Bartunek, J. (2004) Dualities and tensions of planned organisational change, in: S.M. Poole, A. Van de Ven, *Handbook of Organisational Change and Innovation*, pp. 73–107 (Oxford: Oxford University Press).

Snyder, N. and Duarte, D. (2003) *Strategic Innovation: Embedding Innovation as a Core Competency in Your Organisation* (San Francisco, CA: Jossey Bass Business and Management Series).

Starik, M. (1995) Should trees have managerial standing? Toward stakeholder status for non-human nature, *Journal of Business Ethics*, 14, pp. 204–217.

Stern, N. (2006) Stern Review on the Economics of Climate Change, Available at http://www.hmtreasury.gov.uk/independent_reviews/stern_review_economics_climate_change/sternreview_index.cfm (accessed 30 May 2008).

Tregigda, H. and Milne, M. (2006) From sustainable management to sustainable development: a longitudinal analysis of a leading New Zealand environmental reporter, *Business Strategy and the Environment*, 15, pp. 219–241.

Turner, R. K. (1992) Speculations on weak and strong sustainability, Centre for Social and Economic Research on the Global Environment, University of East Anglia and University College London CSERGE WORKING PAPER GEC 92–26. Available at http://www.uea.ac.uk/env/cserge/pub/wp/gec/gec_1992_26.pdf (accessed 26 May 2008)

Uhl-Bien, M., Marion, R. and McKelvey, B. (2007) Complexity leadership theory: shifting leadership from the industrial age to the knowledge era, *The Leadership Quarterly*, 18, pp. 298–318.

Waage, S. (2007) Re-considering product design: a practical 'road-map' for integration of sustainability issues, *Journal of Cleaner Production*, 15, pp. 638–649.

Waddell, D., Cummins, T. and Worley, C. (2007) *Organisation Development and Change*, 3rd edn (South Melbourne: Thomson).

Winn, M. and Zietsma, C. (2004) The war of the woods: a forestry giant seeks peace, *Greener Management International*, 48, pp. 21–37.

York, R. (2004) The treadmill of (diversifying) production, organization & environment, Vol. 17, pp. 355–362.

# A Proposed Model for Evaluating the Sustainability of Continuous Change Programmes

MIKAEL BRÄNNMARK*,** & SUZANNE BENN†

*Royal Institute of Technology (KTH), Stockholm, Sweden, **Linköping University, Sweden, †University of Technology, Sydney, Australia

ABSTRACT *Many studies report that it is difficult to sustain change. This article focuses on how an organization can initiate and sustain a continuous change process. A theoretical model is proposed as a fusion of two previous models for evaluating the sustainability of a change programme; the first is based on analysing stakeholder interest balance as a prerequisite for organizational sustainability, the second on analysing the design of the implementation, indicating whether long-term effects will be achieved. It is argued that the combination of these factors provides a more comprehensive perspective, since it allows us to evaluate both the 'form' and the 'direction' of the programme. To assess stakeholder interest balance, the goal for the change programme is analysed, utilizing the broad stakeholder interest balance perspective. To assess the design of the implementation, four preconditions for long-term effects should be analysed: management's ownership of the change initiative, professional steering, competent leadership and participation. Reference is given to the management concept Lean Production, which is claimed to engage the organization in continuous change. Application of the model highlights the mismatch between narrowly focused change programmes such as Lean Production and sustainable change.*

## Introduction

The vexed issue of the sustainability of a change programme, or in other words, of making change 'stick', is receiving increased attention in both scholarly and practitioner literature (Buchanan *et al.*, 2005; Dunphy *et al* 2007; Doppelt, 2008; Benn and Baker, 2009; Burnes, 2004; 2009). Under pressure from imperatives such as globalization and technological innovation, managers face the knowledge that maintaining change over time is difficult (Beer and Nohria, 2000; Smith, 2002; Knodel, 2004; Burnes, 2004; 2009) and that many such changes decay over time. Maintaining new ways of working and applying them to address the requirements of a rapidly evolving and increasingly complex business context is the real challenge of sustainability (Bateman and David, 2002). For while there is an increased pressure on organizations to shift from traditional bureaucratic structures to more flexible and adaptive forms of organization, these new, more flexible organization structures should not necessarily be seen as replacements to the traditional organizational form. Rather, as Graetz and Smith (2009) point out, they can be viewed as complementary and fulfilling different needs.

One example of a 'new' form for organizing is the Toyota-inspired management concept of Lean Production (Womack *et al.*, 1991; Hines *et al.*, 2004; Pettersen, 2009), increasingly influential in the manufacturing industry (Börnfelt, 2006; Johansson and Abrahamsson, 2009). While Lean can take on many forms, continuous improvement is often argued to be a key aspect of the concept (Pettersen, 2009). The success of Lean rests on the organization continuously changing itself through smaller and larger changes, and thus, the means to facilitate these changes is needed. Using Weick and Quinn's (1999) terminology, and based on this interpretation of Lean, the concept can be characterized as advocating *continuous* rather than *episodic* change. However, introduction of the Lean concept itself could be viewed as a form of episodic change, leading to continuous change when the concept is assimilated into the organization. In using Lean as an example of continuous change, one shoud be mindful that it has been criticized on the grounds that it does not progress wider organizational learning, is perhaps only relevant to the high volume and routinized workplace such as the automobile industry and does not necessarily address the concerns of other organizational stakeholders (Hines *et al.*, 2004). This article seeks to develop a model for the evaluation of continuous change which would assist in overcoming these limitations.

The specific evaluation of such a continuous change programme creates important challenges. The reason for this is that organizational change is often evaluated after the change programme has been completed, that is, it is evaluated as an episodic change. This raises the question of how to evaluate the sustainability of a change programme, such as Lean, intended on initiating an organizational state which is characterized by continuous change and thus lacks an end-state.

This article contributes to the theory and practice of change management by proposing a multifactorial model for evaluating the sustainability of an organization's continuous change processes. In doing so, an attempt is made to clarify the semantic confusion around 'sustainable change'.

## Defining 'Sustainable Change'

The term 'sustainability' is difficult to define in a universal manner. The challenge for scholars and practitioners is that as the importance of sustainability has spread across both management theory and practice so has the confusion surrounding its definition (Garriga and Mele, 2004). In the *change management* literature, sustainable change is taken as meaning change that 'sticks' or becomes the new norm in the organization (e.g. Drew *et al.*, 2004; Bateman and David, 2002; Buchanan *et al.*, 2005). The concept is also applied in the context of *sustainable work systems*, also sometimes referred to as 'regenerative work'. Such work requires work systems that regenerate the resources of the employees, rather than diminish them, contributing to the development of both human and social resources (e.g. Svensson *et al.*, 2007; Kira and Forslin, 2008; Docherty *et al.*, 2009; Zink *et al.*, 2009). It is acknowledged that in the discourse of *sustainable development*, 'sustainable' is interpreted to refer to the balancing of ecological, economical and social factors for future and current generations (World Commission on Environmental and Development (WCED), 1987). However, it is beyond the scope of this article to specifically aim to address sustainability from this macro perspective. The article seeks to recommend an approach to ongoing change that meets the meso level needs of a sustainable work system. However, a wider definition of stakeholder, is incorporated that also encompasses the shareholder, the wider community and the natural environment itself (e.g. Starik and Rands, 1995; Driscoll and Starik, 2004; Haigh and Griffiths, 2009).

This article argues that the concept of *stakeholder interest balance*, which is often used in the literature of change management (e.g. Beer and Nohria, 2000), could be usefully deployed to link the different interpretations of change that 'stick' and sustainable work systems. In doing so, it extends Eklund's (1998) argument for a connection between stakeholder interest balance and organizational sustainability, where the interests of the main stakeholders (employers, customers and employees) of the organization need to be balanced. It is proposed that the durability of a sustainable change programme derives from the programme's commitment to the ongoing renewal and regeneration of employee resources. Building a 'social licence to operate' in the wider community and strategies to ensure that the change programme does not deplete the environmental resources upon which the organization ultimately depends also confers durability and resilience. It is accepted therefore that a sustainable change may not be understood by practitioners as the same as a successful change; whether a change programme is successful or not is mostly determined by the degree of more immediate goal-fulfilment (Rapp, 2002). The key feature of a truly sustainable change must be renewal and regeneration – of other stakeholder organizations, of individual employees and of society and the biosphere. With Dunphy *et al.* (2007), it is argued that some change programmes will play out the features of *sustaining* change while others may be limited by a more efficiency or compliance based approach, where stakeholders representing financial or regulatory control may be prioritized.

This leads to the suggestion that stakeholder interest balance is a plausible way to link the different perspectives of 'sustainable'. By taking the broad stakeholder view in measuring stakeholder impact, how a change programme will influence the sustainability of the work system can be approximated, as well as how the programme might meet the wider concerns of sustainable development. The article suggests that this multi-stakeholder perspective to the change initiative defines the durability of the programme, in effect, arguing that measuring stakeholder impact provides a proxy for stakeholder interest balance and therefore the extent to which different stakeholder needs are addressed.

### Sustaining Continuous Change Processes

When evaluating the potential impact from a change programme introducing continuous change, several important distinctions are important to keep in mind.

First, there is a difference in the strategies required for *creating* as compared with *sustaining* or maintaining change (Drew *et al.*, 2004; Meyer and Stensaker, 2006). For example, a 'bottom up' strategy for organizational change can be an effective way of *creating* organizational change (Svensson and von Otter, 2001). There is debate in the literature, however, as to whether the change thus created may be less likely to become lasting. On the one hand, employees often lack the resources and authority to maintain the introduced changes (Svensson *et al.*, 2007), yet on the other hand, widespread engagement is clearly an important factor (Benn and Baker, 2009). It is also necessary to differentiate between intended and unintended, on the one hand, and discrete and continuous change, on the other hand. Whether the change has an objective, in the form of goal(s), a vision or a concept such as Lean Production, distinguishes an *intended* change process from an *unintended* one (Seo *et al.*, 2004). As such, a change with an intention to fulfil a goal, aim or vision, could be described as having an *implementation phase*. An implementation could also be meant to initiate continuous change process, striving towards a goal or vision, meaning a set of interlinked change processes, rather than a single discrete change. This article focuses on changes that aim at initiating continuous change processes.

The article also stresses that not all implementations are expected to initiate a continuous change process; they may have the goal of creating a permanent or temporary change in the form of a discrete change. Conversely, simply because a continuous change has been initiated, the discrete changes created by the process are not necessarily permanent. In fact, the created discrete change cannot always be lasting if the continuous change process is to be sustainable (Buchanan *et al.*, 2005). It is also noted that recent research on complexity leadership argues that sustainable change is in fact discontinuous (Boyatzis, 2006). Thus, the issue here is that the introduced changes are maintained and kept during appropriate periods, given the organizational context and goals of the

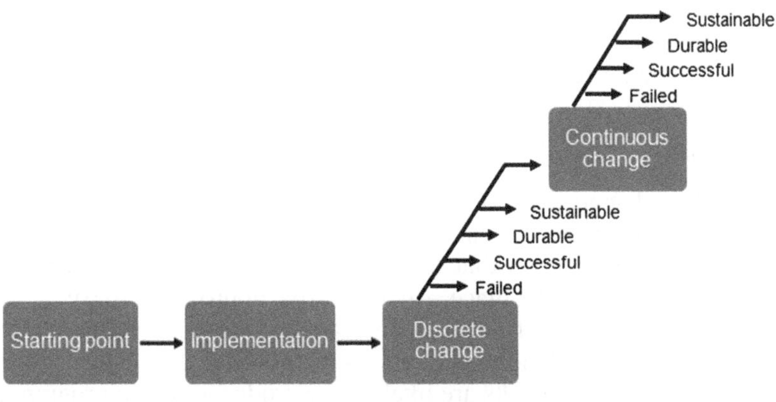


**Figure 1.** The development process.

continuous change process (Buchanan *et al.*, 2005). Another way of putting this point is to say that 'sustainability' is not a static but a dynamic concept (Docherty *et al.*, 2009).

Figure 1 sets out the development process of continuous change. An implementation is meant to either initiate a discrete or a continuous change, although a continuous change process is always preceded by a discrete change. However, this discrete change, e.g. introducing a new procedure for continuous change, is not necessarily the same as the implementation of that change. An implementation could consist of activities such as training in the new procedure, or lectures to justify the need for the new procedure. Consequently, the inclusion of the implementation phase in Figure 1 is important, especially from the point of evaluating the effects of the change programme, because the consequences from this phase could very well differ greatly from the consequences of the continuous or discrete change process itself.

For instance, in the literature regarding the effects of Lean Production on work conditions, Landsbergis *et al.* (1999) note that in the case of two companies they studied, the employees felt satisfied with the high participation during the implementation phase. However, this level of employee participation was not maintained after the system was operating. Research also indicates it is important to understand that the conditions and outcomes of the implementation phase could influence the legitimacy of the long-term continuous change process (Meyer and Stensaker, 2006). For instance, if employees perceive that management's commitment to the change programme is lacking, their engagement in the change process is likely to diminish, making it difficult or even impossible to continue the change programme. This is a common experience in the work with quality circles (Lawler and Mohrman, 1985).

## Evaluating Sustainability

The article now moves from the issue of defining what is meant by sustainable change, to discussing how it could be evaluated in a programme intended on implementing continuous change process. It is argued that, given their importance for sustainability, two factors are highly important to evaluate: the goals of the change programme, i.e. the programme's *direction* (what the programme seeks to achieve) and the *implementation strategy* used (how the programme seeks to implement the sought results).

### *Goal Evaluation*

Evaluation of a change programme can be done retrospectively (i.e. after the change is done) or during the change process. The problem with both of these approaches is that they mean that the change programme needs to be initiated before an evaluation can take place. An alternative approach is to try to 'approximate' the likely outcome of the change programme before it is initiated. One such way, as discussed further below, is to assess the goals of the change programme, since they indicate which results are likely to be produced by the programme. For a change programme meant to initiate a continuous change process, it is difficult to evaluate it retrospectively (although it could be done during the programme's duration), specifically because it is assumed to be continuous, and at least in theory, to have no real endpoint. This suggests that the most appropriate approach is to evaluate the goals and intents behind the change programme, to approximate its potential stakeholder interest impact, and thus, the programme's likely effect on the sustainability of the work system as well as on the wider range of stakeholders such as the natural environment.

In support of the argument that the goals of a change programme can be a viable way of assessing the likely outcome, several researchers have noted that the likely organizational outcome of a change programme does not depend solely upon the specific change programme concept itself but that management's intentions are also important (Westphal *et al.*, 1997; Poksinska *et al.*, 2002; Brulin and Svensson, 2011). With the implementation of ISO 9000, for example, if management is mainly seeking to implement the quality management system for the sake of an ISO-certification, then this is also what they most likely will receive – and only this. However, if they instead try to use the standards as a continuation of their work with quality management, i.e. an approach more in line with the 'philosophy' behind the standard, they are more likely to achieve efficiency gains from the implementation of ISO 9000 (Poksinska *et al.*, 2002). As well, organizations that implement the TQM concept largely as a management fad or to gain legitimacy gains from their customers, are less likely to receive efficiency gains than those organizations who try to reflect upon how the concept fits them, and how it can be best adapted to suit their needs and goals (Westphal *et al.*, 1997). These studies are therefore supportive of the argument that *why* an organization initiates a change programme is as important as *which* change programme they initiate. In other words, they suggest that management's reasons for the change programme are likely to be as important as the programme itself, because the intended goals affect the likely outcome of the programme.

### *The Implementation Design*

While the goals of the change programme are highly important to evaluate, since they likely approximate the potential outcome of the programme, *the design of the implementation* is also a key factor. In this section, it is suggested that Svensson *et al.*'s (2007) model for organizing a change project in such a way that it leads to management's sought *long-term effects* (as contrasted to short-term *results*), from the change programme, is useful to evaluate the organizational features of the implementation phase (Figure 2).

There are two reasons for this. First, because organizations *introducing* a new organizational structure or the means to work with continuous change are being discussed, e.g. continuous improvements. Thus, the continuous change process is preceded by an implementation phase, which affects the sustainability of the continuous change process, as already argued. Hence, it is necessary to also evaluate the design of the implementation, because an ill-designed implementation could ruin the chances of creating a sustainable continuous change process. However, as discussed above, management's goal for the changes predict the likely outcome of the programme. Consequently, if the continuous change

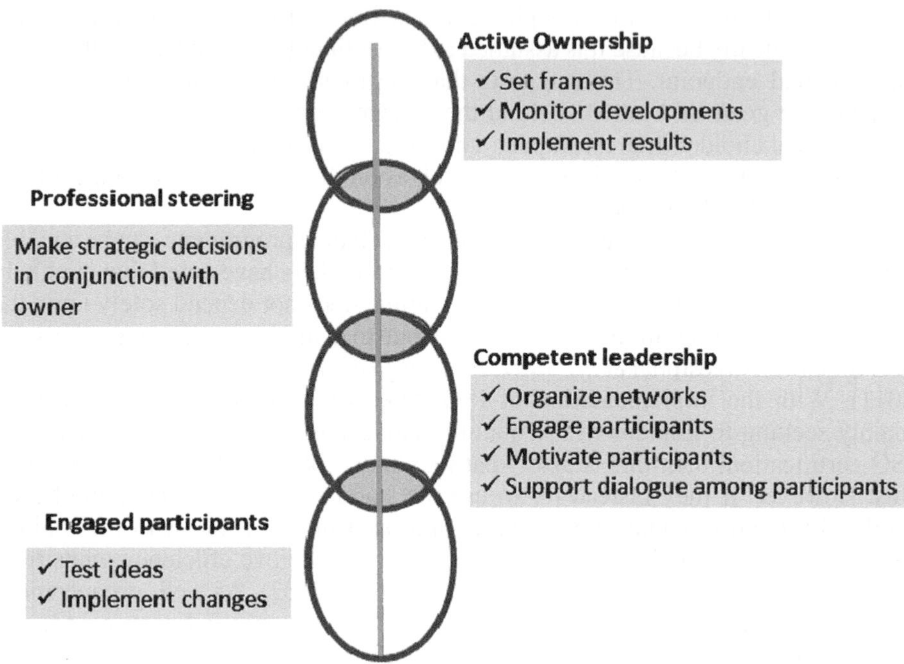


**Figure 2.** Enablers for sustainability (reproduced with permission from Halvarsson and Öhman-Sandberg, 2009).

process is to be sustainable, management's goals of the change programme must be balanced from the perspective of the stakeholders of the organization, recognizing that from a sustainable development viewpoint, stakeholder impact must be assessed from the perspective of the long-term impact of the change on the broader socio-ecological system (Clifton and Amran, 2011). If they are, and the organization uses an implementation design close to Svensson *et al.*'s (2007) model, this would arguably allow both a successful implementation phase followed by a high chance of goal-fulfilment, and thus, a sustainable continuous change process.

Svensson *et al.*'s (2007) model uses four enablers for *long-term effects*: management ownership of the change initiative, professional steering, competent leadership and engaged participants. Each of the enablers is also referred to by other researchers in this field, supporting the claim for inclusion in this model. First, *active ownership* of the implementation, meaning owner and top management commitment and involvement in the change project is highly important for creating long-term effects (Norrgren *et al.*, 1996; Bateman, 2005; Dunphy *et al.*, 2007; Svensson *et al.*, 2007;). Svensson *et al.* (2007) also stress the importance of having an *active* owner of the change programme in the top management, who can take responsibility for the results and make sure that they are implemented in the organization.

Second, *professional steering* of a change programme is important if change is going to 'stick' (Knodel, 2004; Bateman, 2005; Svensson *et al.*, 2007). An example of this is a steering group, which can overlook the implementation process, allocate resources when needed and make sure that the implementation is meeting the ongoing needs of the owners (Svensson *et al.*, 2007). Another example could be a method for visualizing and steering the project work (Knodel, 2004) or the appointment of a coordinator or 'change agent' for sustaining continuous improvement activities (Bateman, 2005). Active feedback for those involved in the implementation is another very important steering aspect (Norrgren *et al.*, 1996).

Third, *continuing and competent leadership* is highly important for successful organizational change in order to act as inspirers and to 'lead by example'. This has been stressed by many authors (Kotter, 1996; Aoki, 2008; Svensson *et al.*, 2007; Taylor *et al.*, 2011; Whelan-Berry and Somerville, 2010). However, a number of writers (Ibarra and Hunter, 2007; Svensson *et al.*, 2007) also point to the leader's importance for partnering, networking and creating a dialogue between all of those involved in or impacted by the project, including those often perceived as fringe stakeholders (Hart and Sharma, 2004), such as groups representing the natural environment, for instance. Partnering and networking enables learning and change, particularly applying to partnerships between NGOs and corporations in connection with their strategic sustainability activities (Porter and Kramer, 2006; Matten and Moon, 2008). Lastly, *engaged participants*, who can act as local inspirers and also add momentum and ensure commitment to the change, are highly important for sustainability (Boyatzis, 2006; Svensson *et al.*, 2007). From the perspective of sustainable change, engaging participants may involve engaging fringe stakeholders in order to both pre-empt stakeholder concerns and provide innovative suggestions to the dilemmas of organizations attempting to reposition themselves via new structures or implementing reforms such as Lean (Hart and Sharma, 2004). Another way of putting this issue is to highlight the importance of allowing all affected by the change to *participate* in the implementation. But they also need to be empowered to participate in the implementation through provision of resources such as time, skills and training (Kotter, 1996; Norrgren *et al.*, 1996; Rapp, 2002; Bateman, 2005; Whelan-Berry and Somerville, 2010). Kotter (1996) refers to this as the importance of 'empowerment'. For example, researchers have shown that certain human resource management policies and practices can facilitate change through prompting employee engagement with environmental programmes (Ramus and Steger, 2000).

Halvarsson and Öhman-Sandberg (2009) develop Svensson *et al.*'s (2007) model arguing that the four enablers of ownership, steering, leadership and engaged participants interact with each other and that therefore there is a need for communication and coordination between them. They refer to *structural* factors, such as visions and goals for the change, together with *process* factors, such as how learning is facilitated during the development process. For instance, goals and visions are the sought consequences of a change programme, which then need steering together with learning processes and engaged participants, and competent leadership, using feedback to monitor their progress, to assure that the change initiative is developing in accordance with the goals and vision.

Consequently, Svensson *et al.*'s (2007) model, as further developed by Halvarsson and Öhman-Sandberg (2009), is meant to increase the chance of organizations achieving sought long-term effects, i.e. a form of goal-fulfilment. When this model is, in turn, combined with Eklund's (1998) model, where the goals are used to approximate the impact on the stakeholder interest balance from the change programme, Figure 3 is derived.

Thus, management's goal for a change programme are more likely to be achieved if an implementation design similar to the one proposed by Svensson *et al.* (2007) is used. Consequently, the implementation design *and* management's goal are evaluated, it is possible to approximate (though far from predict, of course) whether: (1) the programme has a likely chance of achieving the sought goals, and (2) how the introduced changes (as guided by the goals of management) changes the stakeholder interest balance in the organization. Arguably then, when these two factors are put together, the sustainability of a change programme meant to introduce continuous change can be estimated.

## Discussion

In considering the aim of this article to develop a model to evaluate the sustainability of programmes aimed at implementing continuous change processes, it is acknowledged that this model is only a proposal, based on previous research and theoretical models. One could argue that it is overambitious to try to evaluate the 'sustainability' of a programme mean to initiate continuous change processes at the levels proposed here, i.e. from the perspectives of change 'stickiness', as well as of regenerative work, systems. This is, however, an empirical question, rather than a theoretical one. Thus, in order to empirically and methodologically *validate* the proposed model according to these different levels of sustainability, considerable future research is needed.

In each instance, this would best be done by using a longitudinal approach, sampling either qualitative or quantitative data at several separate points in time from the studied organization(s). One alternative to this more extensive approach would be to try to assess how 'robust' the model is for evaluating sustainability by assessing stakeholder interest balance and enablers for long-term effects. For instance, this could be done using several case studies, pooling the results and thus calculating the chance of the model giving valid conclusions.

While the focus of this article has been to evaluate sustainability of a continuous change process, e.g. the introduction of Lean Production, this model can likely be used to evaluate programmes meant to introduce discrete change as well. Given the special nature of a continuous change process (which is the focus and interest of this article), i.e. that they are (at least in theory) meant to have no real endpoint in time, this means that retrospective methods (which are available for discrete change) cannot be used for a continuous change process. However, one could evaluate the process during it's progress, though there are two potential problems with this. First of all, this will mean that the change programme needs to be initiated. Second, an evaluation of the process takes time, meaning that it either needs to be halted, or that the process risks having moved on to a point such that when the evaluation is finished, the conclusions from it may no longer be

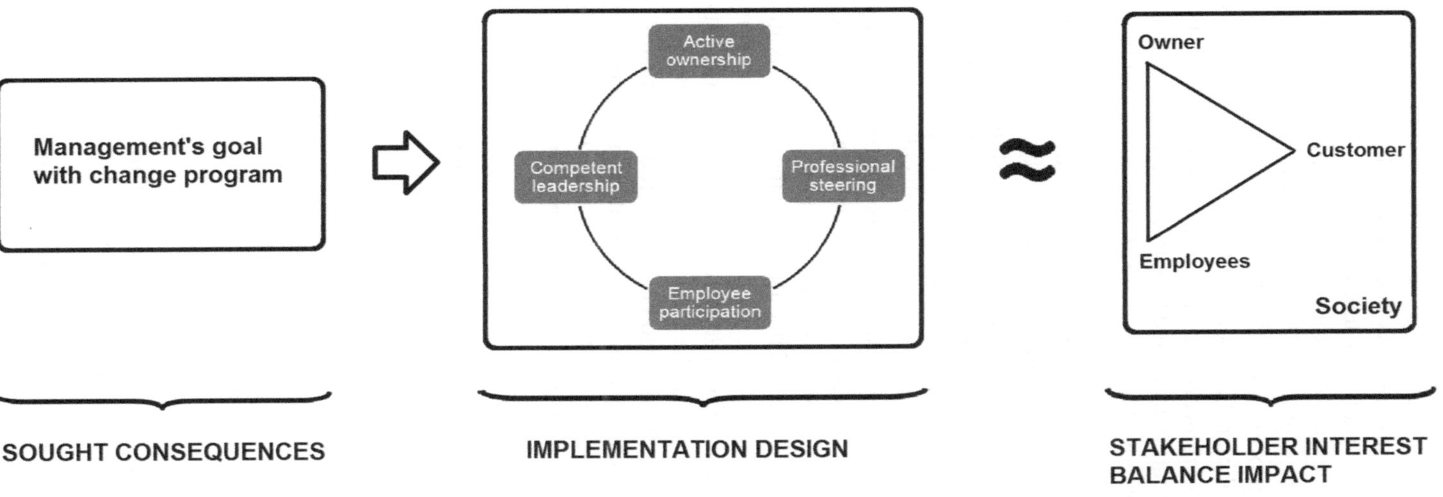


**Figure 3.** Evaluative Model (modified with permission from Eklund, 1998; Svensson *et al.*, 2007; Halvarsson and Öhman-Sandberg, 2009).

of relevance. Consequently, from the perspective of risk management and potential resource usage, assessing the change before it is initiated does offer an advantage compared to after the process has been initiated.

However, given the importance of learning and process feedback for creating durable change and achieving the sought long-term effects of a change programme, it is plausible to argue for the need of a continuous evaluation during the continuous change process as well (Norrgren *et al.*, 1996; Svensson *et al.*, 2007; Halvarsson and Öhman-Sandberg, 2009; Brulin and Svensson, 2011), i.e. different means for *learning evaluations* (e.g. Brulin *et al.*, 2009). Consequently, these approaches to evaluating a change programme are not mutually exclusive to, or a substitute for, the proposed model. Instead, they are a highly important complement to it.

One advantage of the proposed model arises from its ability to evaluate two distinct aspects of the question of sustainability: management's goals or the sought stakeholder interest balance consequences, and the design of the implementation, meaning if the implementation is likely to lead to the intended consequences. These features of the model reduce the risk of creating a one-sided (and possibly misleading) result, thereby arguably increasing the likely validity of the results from the model. Consequently, if the model shows favourable results regarding both the direction and the design of the implementation, this indicates a higher chance of creating a sustainable continuous change process, while if only one of them shows positive results, the chance is likely lower. This aspect of the model is highly important, since influence from 'external' factors, such as a consulting company's change programme initiated in an organization, can provide an 'illusion' of sustainability, if the evaluative model solely focuses on the implementation design.

This aspect of the model should also be considered as a means of reducing the risk of researchers and managers blindly following a newly popular management concept, such as Lean Production. For instance, it is not uncommon in the Lean literature that the advocates of the concept promise many tempting results and effects from the implementation of Lean – some even arguing for the introduction of Lean in all companies in order to benefit society more widely (Womack *et al.*, 1991). However, while one cannot, of course, completely rule out that a concept such as Lean will often produce certain effects, based on the previous referred to studies and argumentation in this article, it is argued here that the effects of a Lean implementation will as likely depend on the management's goal and the implementation design, as on the concept itself. Evaluating management's goal for the change programme can to some degree predict the effects the programme will produce (if an appropriate organization for the implementation is used). In addressing theoretically the question of whether some management concepts are likely to produce sustainable change than others, the model suggests that sustainability does not depend upon the specifics of the chosen concept. Instead, it depends mostly on other factors, i.e. the design of the implementation in terms of its structure and processes and management goals for the concept, rather than the chosen concept itself.

Many of the factors used and argued for in project management are *temporary* in nature, given that they are based on projects. Therefore, it is relevant to ask if these types of steering systems, such as a steering group, are appropriate for use in the implementation of continuous change programmes such as Lean Production. One could argue that they work well during the implementation phase; however, this means that the organization needs to find other forms for steering after this phase is over. Conversely, one could argue that organizations instead should immediately integrate the work with the concept in their ordinary management and steering structures. Therefore, one could further argue that a temporary steering system makes for an easier implementation phase and conversely, that integrating the work into the ordinary management systems will mean less momentum during the implementation, although this could avoid the difficulties of moving from an implementation phase into the long-term continuous change process. However, if Graetz and Smith's (2009) argumentation is accepted, this is actually a non-issue; instead, according to these researchers, these types of temporary steering structures should exist side by side with the ordinary management structures, since they complement each other. This approach is more in line with recent interpretations of change that lend themselves to open dialogue and questioning and have the potential to facilitate strategic direction setting in the face of complexity and ambiguity (Clegg *et al.*, 2007). Also, from the perspective of Eklund's (1998) and Svensson *et al*'s (2007) models, the advantage of these types of temporary steering mechanisms is that they likely provide a forum for correcting the direction of the change programme. Thus, if the organization is aware of the need for stakeholder interest balance, a steering group could be used as a means for representative employee participation and wider stakeholder engagement, thereby providing some means for employee interest fulfilment as well as responding strategically to the needs of fringe stakeholders such as those groups representing the interests of the natural environment (Sharma and Henriques, 2005). Hence it also acts as a means to steer the change programme in a direction towards stakeholder interest balance, taking the broad stakeholder view and therefore addressing the wider needs of a more sustainable development than the narrow inward-looking focus of the continuous improvement traditionally embraced by change programmes such as Lean.

Lastly, while the proposed model uses Svensson *et al*'s (2007) 'enablers' for evaluating the form of the change programme, only longitudinal studies over an extended time period can validate the model. Thus, this model can only *indicate probabilities* for sustainability; it cannot be used to *determine* if an organizational change programme will lead to a sustainable continuous change process within an organization. Of course, one could easily argue that it is by definition impossible to actually 'determine' if a change programme will be sustainable; in the end, only probabilities should be discussed, since many things can occur which could affect the sustainability of the change programme. Again using Svensson *et al*'s (2007) model, and Halvarsson and Öhman-Sandberg's (2009) further development of the model, using an implementation design which has means for steering and learning processes built into the programme likely provide some means to handle this issue.

## Conclusion

Several conclusions can be drawn based on the above discussion . The discussion provides support for the argument that evaluating the sustainability of a change programme should be in terms of both the aimed for direction and the design of the implementation of the change programme. Stakeholder interest balance utilizing the broad stakeholder view is suggested as a concept that allows change to be operationalized so that the different interpretations of 'sustainability' are linked. The extant literature supports the suggestion that management's goal for the change programme is a plausible way of assessing stakeholder interest balance and so provides a means to evaluate the direction of the change programme. The second suggestion, based on the previous models, is that organizational preconditions for achieving management's sought long-term effects from a change programme are professional steering, management's ownership of the change programme, competent leadership and participation for all affected by the change programme. Consequently, it can be concluded that these are suitable ways of evaluating the design of the implementation.

The proposed model evaluates all of these factors, i.e. it assesses both the direction and the design of the change programme. Therefore, the overall conclusion here is that the proposed model is theoretically viable. The next step is to present a way to operationalize the model, and consequently provide a means for testing the validity and robustness of the model. This is a good basis for future research that may enable the recognized sustainability limitations of narrow understandings of continuous change programmes, such as Lean Production, to be overcome.

## References


Aoki, K. (2008) Transferring Japanese kaizen activities to overseas plants in China, *International Journal of Operations & Production Management*, 28(6), pp. 518–539.

Bateman, N. (2005) Sustainability: the elusive element of process improvements, *International Journal of Operations & Production Management*, 25(3), pp. 261–276.

Bateman, N. and David, A. (2002) Process improvements programmes: a model for assessing sustainability, *International Journal of Operations & Production Management*, 22(5), pp. 515–526.

Beer, M. and Nohria, N. (2000) Cracking the code of change, *Harvard Business Review*, May/June.

Benn, S. and Baker, E. (2009) Advancing Sustainability Through Change and Innovation: A Co-evolutionary Perspective, *Journal of Change Management*, 9(4), pp. 383–397.

Börnfelt, P-O. (2006) Förändringskompetens på industrigolvet, *Arbete och Hälsa*, 1.

Boyatzis, R.E. (2006) An overview of intentional change from a complexity perspective, *Journal of Management Development*, 25(7), pp. 607–623.

Brulin, G. and Svensson, L. (2011) *Att äga, styra och utvärdera stora projekt* (Lund: Studentlitteratur AB).

Brulin, G., Svensson, L., Jansson, K. and Sjöberg, K. (2009) *Learning Through Ongoing Evaluation*, pp. 149–166 (Lund: Studentlitteratur).

Buchanan, D., Fitzgerald, L., Ketley, D., Gollop, R., Jones, J.L, Lamont, S.S., Neath, A. and Whitby, E. (2005) No going back: a review of the literature on sustaining organizational change, *International Journal of Management Reviews*, 7(3), pp. 189–205.

Burnes, B. (2004) Emergent change and planned change – competitors or allies?, *International Journal of Operations & Production Management*, 24(9), pp. 886–902.

Burnes, B. (2009) Reflections: ethics and organizational change – Time for a return to Lewinian values, *Journal of Change Management*, 9(4), pp. 359–381.

Clegg, S., Kornberger, M. and Rhodes, C. (2007) Business ethics as practice, *British Journal of Management*, 18(2), pp. 107–122.

Clifton, D. and Amran, A. (2011) The stakeholder approach: a sustainability perspective, *Journal of Business Ethics*, 98(1), pp. 121–136.

Docherty, P., Kira, M. and Shani, A.B.R. (2009) What the world needs now is sustainable work systems, in: P. Docherty, M. Kira and A.B.R. Shani (eds) *Creating Sustainable Work Systems*, pp. 1–22 (London: Routledge).

Doppelt, B. (2008) *Leading Change Toward Sustainability: A Change-Management Guide for Business, Government and Civil Society* (Sheffield: Greenleaf).

Drew, J., McCallum, B. and Roggenhofer, S. (2004) *Journey to Lean: Making Operational Change Stick* (Basingstoke: Palgrave Macmillan).

Driscoll, C. and Starik, M. (2004) The primordial stakeholder: advancing the conceptual consideration of stakeholder status for the natural environment, *Journal of Business Ethics*, 49(1), pp. 55–73.

Dunphy, D., Griffiths, A. and Benn, S. (2007) *Organizational Change for Corporate Sustainability*, 2nd edn (London: Routledge).

Eklund, J. (1998) Work conditions and company strategies, in: P. Vink, E. Koningsveld and S. Dhondt (eds) *Human Factors in Organizational Design and Management – IV*, pp. 263–268 (Amsterdam: North Holland).

Garriga, E. and Mele, D. (2004) Corporate social responsibility theories: mapping the territory, *Journal of Business Ethics*, 53(1/2), pp. 51–71.

Graetz, F. and Smith, A.C.T. (2009) Duality theory and organising forms in change management, *Journal of Change Management*, 9(1), pp. 9–25.

Haigh, N. and Griffiths, A. (2009) The natural environment as a primary stakeholder: the case of climate change, *Business Strategy and the Environment*, 18(6), pp. 347–359.

Halvarsson, A. and Öhman-Sandberg, A. (2009) How theory can contribute to learning – interactive research in national programmes, in: G. Brulin, L. Svensson, K. Jansson and K. Sjöberg (eds) *Learning Through Ongoing Evaluation*, pp. 149–166 (Lund: Studentlitteratur).

Hart, S. and Sharma, S. (2004) Engaging fringe stakeholders for competitive imagination, *Academy of Management Executive*, 18, pp. 8–18.

Hines, P., Holweg, M. and Rich, N. (2004) Learning to evolve: a review of contemporary lean thinking, *International Journal of Operations & Production Management*, 24(10), pp. 994–1011.

Ibarra, H. and Hunter, M. (2007) How leaders build and use networks, *Harvard Business Review*, 85(1), pp. 40–47.

Johansson, J. and Abrahamsson, L. (2009) The good work – a Swedish trade union vision in the shadow of lean production, *Applied Ergonomics*, 40, pp. 775–780.

Kira, M. and Forslin, J. (2008) Seeking regenerative work in the post-bureaucratic transition, *Journal of Organizational Change Management*, 21(1), pp. 76–91.

Knodel, T. (2004) Preparing the organizational 'soil' for measurable and sustainable change: business value management and project governance, *Journal of Change Management*, 4(1), pp. 45–62.

Kotter, J.P. (1996) *Leading Change* (Boston: Harvard Business School Press).

Landsbergis, P.A., Cahill, J. and Schnall, P. (1999) The impact of lean production and related new systems of work organization on worker health, *Journal of Occupational Health Psychology*, 4(2), pp. 108–130.

Lawler, E.E., III and Mohrman, S.A. (1985) Quality circles after the fad, *Harvard Business Review*, January–February.

Matten, D. and Moon, J. (2008) 'Implicit' and 'explicit' CSR: a conceptual framework for a comparative understanding of corporate social responsibility, *Academy of Management Review*, 33, pp. 404–424.

Meyer, C.B. and Stensaker, I.G. (2006) Developing capacity for change, *Journal of Change Management*, 6(2), pp. 217–331.

Norrgren, F., Hart, H. and Schaller, J. (1996) *Förändringsstrategiers Effektivitet*, CORE WP 3 (Gothenburg: Chalmers University of Technology).

Pettersen, J. (2009) Defining Lean Production – some conceptual and practical issues, *The TQM Journal*, 21(2), pp. 127–142.

Poksinska, B., Dahlgaard, J.J. and Antoni, M. (2002) The state of ISO 9000 certification: a study of Swedish organizations, *The TQM Magazine*, 14(5), pp. 297–306.

Porter, M.E. and Kramer, M.R. (2006) Strategy and society: the link between competitive advantage and corporate social responsibility, *Harvard Business Review*, 84(12), pp. 78–92.

Ramus, C.A. and Steger, U. (2000) The roles of supervisory support behaviors and environmental policy in employee 'Ecoinitiatives' at leading-edge European companies, *Academy of Management Journal*, 43(4), pp. 605–626.

Rapp, C. (2002) Exploring the sustainability of improvement activities, Thesis, Linköping University, Linköping Studies in Science and Technology, 950.

Seo, M., Putnam, L. and Bartunek, J. (2004) Dualities and tensions of planned organisational change, in: M.S. Poole and A. Van de Ven (eds) *Handbook of Organisational Change and Innovation*, pp. 73–107 (Oxford: Oxford University Press).

Sharma, S. and Henriques, I. (2005) Stakeholder influences on sustainability practices in the canadian forest products industry, *Strategic Management Journal*, 26(2), pp. 159–180.

Smith, M.E. (2002) Success rates for different types of organizational change, *Performance Improvements*, 41(1), pp. 26–35.

Starik, M. and Rands, G.P. (1995) Weaving an integrated web: multilevel and multisystem perspectives of ecologically sustainable organisations, *Academy of Management Review*, 20(4), pp. 908–935.

Svensson, L., Aronsson, G., Randle, H. and Eklund, J. (2007) *Hållbart arbetsliv – projekt som gästspel eller som hållbar utveckling* (Malmö: Gleerups).

Svensson, L. and von Otter, C. (2001) *Projektarbete – teori och praktik* (Stockholm: Santérus Förlag).

Taylor, A., Cocklin, C., Brown, R. and Wilson-Evered, E. (2011) An investigation of champion-driven leadership processes, *The Leadership Quarterly*, 21(2), pp. 412–433.

Weick, K.E. and Quinn, R.E. (1999) Organizational change and development, *Annual Review of Psychology*, 50, pp. 361–386.

Westphal, J.D., Gulati, R. and Shortell, S.M. (1997) Customization or conformity? An institutional and network perspective on the content and consequences of TQM adoption, *Administrative Science Quarterly*, 42(2), pp. 366–394.

Whelan-Berry, K.S. and Somerville, K.A. (2010) Linking change drivers and the organizational change process: a review and synthesis, *Journal of Change Management*, 10(2), pp. 175–193.

Womack, J.P., Roos, D. and Jones, D.T. (1991) *The Machine That Changed the World – The Story of Lean Production* (New York: Harper Perennial).

World Commission on Environmental and Development (WCED) (1987) *Our Common Future, Brundtland Report* (Oxford: Oxford University Press).

Zink, K.J., Steimle, U. and Fischer, K. (2009) Human factors, business excellence and cooperate sustainability: differing perspectives, joint objectives, in: K. Zink (ed) *Cooperate Sustainability as a Challenge for Comprehensive Management*, pp. 3–18 (Heidelberg: Physica-Verlag).

# Index

For Product Safety Concerns and Information please contact our
EU representative GPSR@taylorandfrancis.com Taylor & Francis
Verlag GmbH, Kaufingerstraße 24, 80331 München, Germany